Romantic California Getaways

Other titles in this series:

Romantic Weekend Getaways:
The Mid-Atlantic States

Romantic Island Getaways:
The Caribbean, Bermuda, and the Bahamas

Romantic Hawaiian Getaways

Romantic California Getaways

Larry Fox
Barbara Radin-Fox

John Wiley & Sons, Inc.
New York • Chichester • Brisbane • Toronto • Singapore

Published by John Wiley & Sons, Inc.

Library of Congress Cataloging-in-Publication Data

Fox, Larry, 1945–
    Romantic California getaways / by Larry Fox, Barbara Radin-Fox.
      p. cm.
    Includes index.
    ISBN 0-471-53999-6 (alk. paper) : $12.95
    1. California—Description and travel—1981—Guide-books.
I. Radin-Fox, Barbara. II. Title.
F859.3.F68   1991
917.9404'53—dc20   91-24758
                                   CIP

ISBN 0-471-53999-6 Paper

Printed in the United States of America

10 9 8 7 6 5 4 3 2 1

Printed and bound by Courier Companies, Inc.

Contents

✪

Chapter Four
The Desert Empire 101

✪

Chapter Five
Murder, Music, Magic, and More 119

✪

Chapter Six
Tales of Three Cities 131

✪

Chapter Seven
The Magnificent Mountains 195

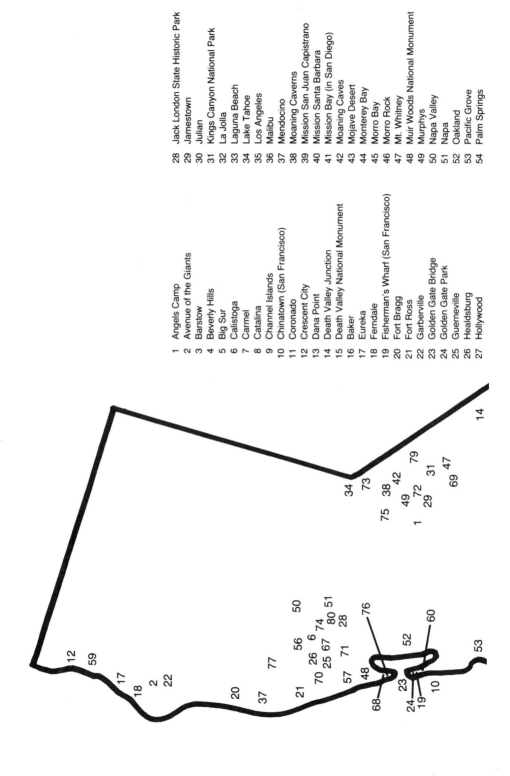

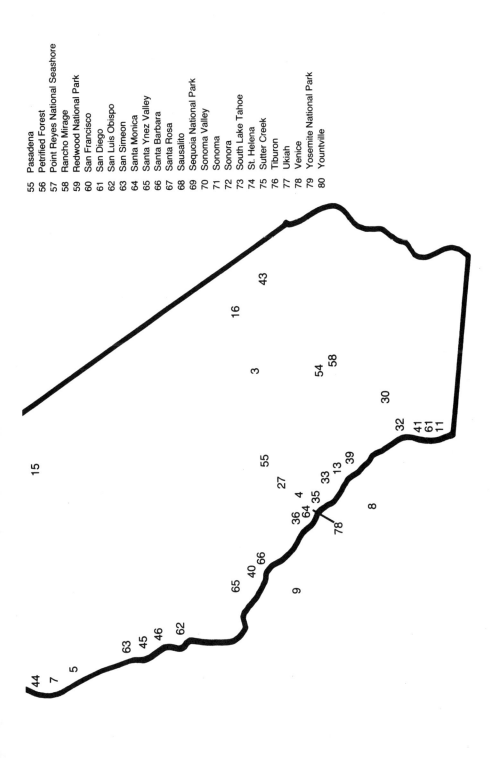

Introduction

From our vantage point in the East, California is the state where dreams come true. Everything we consider romantic can be found here: scenic coasts, stunning mountains, big cities filled with culture and excitement, small towns that showcase the elegance of the past, and a lifestyle that is continually reinventing the art and drama of living well.

Romantic California Getaways guides you on journeys centered around specific themes. These journeys can be getaways for a long weekend or a vacation lasting a week. The chapters explore the wine country, the stunning coastline and the towns and attractions along the shore, those special towns where art is celebrated, the big cities, the mountains and parks, the inns and hotels where you can help solve a mystery or get pampered in luxury, the austerely beautiful desert, and the places where you can find new challenges in sports and adventures. At the end of each chapter, we list intimate inns, fine restaurants, annual festivals, and helpful telephone numbers for the areas in which you will travel.

The places we describe were selected because we found them to be exceptional in beauty, quality, location, or atmosphere. This means we have left out some familiar places—big hotels, famous but unimaginative restaurants, and ordinary museums—because they were not found to be conducive to romance.

Our guide assumes that, with the exception of the big cities, you are touring by car. Before you go, a few tips to make your travel easier:

✪ Get a good map of California and the area you are visiting. The tourist offices/visitors centers we list can help provide you with the maps and other information, such as exact dates and times of festivals. The California Office of Tourism will give you general information on attractions. Contact them at the Department of Commerce, 1121 L Street, Suite 103, Sacramento, CA 95814 (800/862-2543, extension 99).

✪ Inns and bed and breakfasts are often booked weeks (in some cases months) ahead of time. Always make your reservations early if you want to stay at a specific inn or hotel. Reservations are usually required at the better restaurants although you can wait to make them closer to your trip.

✪ Smokers are no longer popular guests in many small inns. If you are a smoker, ask about the rules of the house. Some inns may prefer you stay elsewhere.

✪ You may be faced with a choice to share a bath at some of the inns. If this is a potential problem, be certain the innkeeper knows that you want only a room with a private bath and, if you are sending in a deposit, get it in writing.

✪ The restaurants we selected are chosen on the basis of their dinner menus. Menus and prices for lunch may differ markedly.

✪ Nightlife, particularly good places to dance to romantic music, is hard to find in smaller communities. We have wasted countless hours looking for such places. In this guide, the only sections on nightlife are in the major cities, although exceptional nightspots in smaller communities will be mentioned when warranted.

The inns, hotels, restaurants, and attractions we have selected for this guide are very special, for they have warmed our hearts. Before you go, remember that romance is not a destination; it is that undefinable something that you have in your heart long before you begin to plan and pack for a trip. The trips offered here, however, can help you unlock that mystery and wonder.

LARRY FOX
BARBARA RADIN-FOX

Chapter One

Very Special Places

Romance needs a setting, a place of overpowering beauty that stirs emotions and accentuates feelings. The perfect romantic place is where the glorious works of nature are complemented by creations of man.

California is rich in both. Within its borders are vistas of stunning beauty, natural wonders so breathtaking that they have become famous through photographs and works of art. Then there are the constructed attractions—quaint villages, majestic cities, and elegant resorts. When the two come together, you have a very special place.

There are five villages on California's coast that marry striking natural scenery with outstanding inns and resorts, superb restaurants, and countless galleries of art. These five—Carmel, Laguna Beach, La Jolla, Mendocino, and Santa Barbara—offer different getaways. Mendocino looks like a village on the coast of Maine or Cape Cod. Laguna Beach and La Jolla are contemporary ocean-front communities offering fine art and much more. Carmel is a fantasylike town of inns and boutiques often shrouded in fog and Santa Barbara has never forgotten its Spanish heritage even while enjoying the growth of the 20th century.

Each of these five towns is very wonderful and very romantic in its own individual way.

✪ CARMEL

Carmel is on a bay that author Robert Louis Stevenson called "the most beautiful meeting of land and sea on earth." It's hard to argue with him. Carmel (also called Carmel-by-the-Sea) is a beautiful village on the Monterey Peninsula whose streets are shaded by cypresses and evergreens and colored by numerous hanging baskets and window boxes filled with flowers.

Known as a walker's paradise, Carmel's graceful streets are home to more than 100 art galleries, boutiques, shops, inns, and restaurants. The architectural styles of its homes and buildings range from Mediterranean to Old England. Like the small community that it is, the ambiance and pace is unhurried. There are no numbers on the buildings, no intrusive business signs, few street lights, and, on some side streets, not even sidewalks.

Carmel's heritages—Spanish and art—can be viewed at two historic sites in town: the Carmel Mission and the Tor House. The Carmel Mission, founded in 1770 by Father Junipero Serra, is at Rio Road and Lausen Drive on the south side of town. Father Serra is buried on the grounds of the mission (formally called the Mission San Carlos Borromeo del Rio Carmelo). It has been restored and offers displays on the church's early years. In addition, the basilica is a very popular place for weddings.

Carmel's more recent artistic heritage is illustrated at the Tor House, the home of poet Robinson Jeffers (26304 Ocean View

✪ The windswept beach at lovely Carmel, on the Monterey Peninsula. (Dane Thompson)

Avenue). Docents lead tours of this unusual oceanfront home. The outside retaining wall contains lava from Hawaii, rocks from the Temple of Heaven in Peking, and pieces of the Great Wall of China.

The main thoroughfare of Carmel is Ocean Avenue. It offers a host of galleries, shops, and restaurants. The choices can be overwhelming, but do see the bronze sculptures at the Bennett Sculpture Gallery at Ocean and Juniper avenues, the works of Ansel Adams and other (lesser) photographers at the Photography West Gallery at Ocean Avenue and Dolores Street, or contemporary folk art at the Bill W. Dodge Gallery on Dolores Street between Fifth and Sixth streets. In the same block as the Dodge Gallery are Carmel Art Associates, which features Southwestern art, and the Fireside Gallery, for ceramics and etchings. Other nice shops include the New Masters Gallery (works by more than 60 artists) on Sixth Avenue near San Carlos, Peter Rabbit and Friends (books, music boxes, and other items from Beatrix Potter's books) on Lincoln Avenue between Seventh and Ocean avenues, and the Cottage Gallery (paintings and sculpture) at Mission Street and Sixth Avenue.

Carmel is also the site of other cultural activities. The basilica of the Carmel Mission is home to the candlelight concerts of the 50-year-old Bach Festival every July. The Sunset Community Cultural Center on San Carlos Avenue between Eighth and Ninth streets offers concerts, dance, and shows by star performers throughout the year.

Carmel's location on the sea shapes its plentiful and colorful vegetation as well as contributes to its climate, which is usually cooler than that found a few miles inland. Another contribution from the sea is the frequent fog. One of our favorite memories of this town was when we stopped on one side street and looked back at Ocean Avenue. There we saw a breathtaking surrealistic scene: a low-lying fog cloud moving quickly along the street, enveloping the strollers and playing hide-and-seek with the houses and trees of the town.

The Pacific Ocean and Carmel Beach are found at the west end of Ocean Avenue. The beach is for walking and photography—but not swimming. The water is usually too cold and the surf too rough. The twisted cypresses along the scenic road paralleling the shore and the rocky shore and tidal pools at the south end of the beach offer some interesting photographic possibilities.

Scenic Drive leads south to the 106-acre Carmel River State Beach, where swimming is allowed in the river lagoon. The peninsula in the distance to the south of the beach is Point Lobos State Reserve, a 1,250-acre wilderness offering trails through a cypress forest to the sea. The Sea Lion Point Trail in the park takes you to a lookout where otters, sea lions, and seals may be viewed.

There are two exceptional drives in the area. Carmel Valley Road, which runs inland off Highway 1 south of Carmel, takes you past ranches and the Chateau Julien Winery (stop to taste their chardonnays and sauvignons blancs) before coming to Carmel Valley Village, a small community that is home to even more arts and crafts galleries.

The most striking scenery in the area is found along 17-Mile Drive, which can be entered off Highway 1 and North San Antonio Avenue. The drive costs $5 per car to enter and goes past some of the most magnificent scenery in California. The trees and shrubbery are rough, sculpted into strange shapes by wind and sea. But they are beautiful nonetheless. The Lone Cypress, that twisted tree standing as a lonely sentinel on a rocky finger pointing into the sea, remains a poignant and moving natural wonder. Other famous attractions include Seal Rock and Bird Rock, islands named after their inhabitants. In addition, the drive goes past Pebble Beach Golf Links, a world-famous course, and stupendously beautiful mansions.

Don't let the $5 toll turn you away. The 17-Mile Drive is a road unlike any other in the nation. It's an inexpensive escape into a world of beauty and magnificence.

❂ LAGUNA BEACH

The Spaniards and the Mexicans never really understood that the steep cliffs and rugged canyons that make up Laguna Beach have their own sort of beauty. Those early settlers rejected this part of the southern California coast, preferring to claim or issue grants to more benign lands to the north and south.

Centuries later, it took an artist, Norman St. Clair, to recognize that the steep cliffs, miles of lovely beaches, balmy sunny climate, and striking vegetation were a paradise for artists. St. Clair was the first, but not the last artist to make Laguna Beach his studio. In time he was joined by William Alexander Griffith, William Wendt, and Anna Hills, among others.

Today their heritage can be seen in Orange County's oldest museum—Laguna Art Museum (307 Cliff Drive)—and the more than 60 art galleries that populate the streets of this upscale beach resort. The arts also play a major role in the town's festivals. Arts and crafts are celebrated at the Winter Festival of the Arts in February, the Art-a-Fair in July is a juried show drawing entries worldwide and the Sawdust Festival in July features works by more than 200 artists. The biggest area event, though, is the Festival of Arts and Pageant of the Masters in July and August. In this festival, the works of local artists are displayed, while more than 400 live models (usually local residents) posing in carefully designed backgrounds re-create famous works of art.

The galleries that encourage these celebrations can be found everywhere in town. Among our favorites are the Engman International Gallery, contemporary art (326 Glenneyre Street and 1492 South Coast Highway), the Laguna Beach Gallery of Photography (303 Broadway), Pacific Edge, paintings and serigraphs (206 North Coast Highway), Sun Stone Gallery, early California art (422 North Coast Highway), and the Miranda Galleries, contemporary art (417 South Coast Highway).

Art is not the only attraction in this ocean resort. The area has excellent beaches: Laguna Beach Memorial Park (Pacific Coast Highway and Broadway, in the center of the town), Aliso Beach (Pacific Coast Highway and Crown Valley Parkway), and Crystal Cove State Park (Pacific Coast Highway and Cameo Shores Road).

Other nearby attractions include the lovely mission at San Juan Capistrano. The mission was founded in 1776, and is a fascinating living museum to the life and times of its founder, Father Junipero Serra. The only remaining piece from the original stone church is the wall near the fountain. The church, often called the most magnificent of the 21 missions in the state, was destroyed by an earthquake in 1812.

This mission, though, is famous for a more secular reason. Every March 19 (St. Joseph's Day), the swallows return to Capistrano and the mission. Throughout the mission, the mud-daubed cones that the swallows call home can be found under the eaves and along the rooflines of the buildings.

A fine way to end a day or a visit to Laguna Beach is to drive south on the Coast Highway to the fabulous new Ritz-Carlton in Laguna Niguel. There, you can take part in the sophisticated high tea in the Library or the Lounge. We enjoyed the Lounge, where the huge windows presented us with striking views of the fabulous sunsets.

As the day ends, take a walk on the meticulously landscaped

grounds filled with colorful flowers to the gazebo on the bluff. From this point, you may watch the surfers seeking their perfect wave, catch a glimpse of the whales that migrate in these waters from December to March, or stand in awe at some of the finest sunsets in the world.

✪ LA JOLLA

La Jolla, the coastal community 15 minutes north of downtown San Diego, is a paradise. Picture a curving hillside rising above the blue Pacific. At water's edge are several graceful coves with lovely white sand beaches. Along the hillside are beautiful homes and grand mansions, and near the point dividing the beaches is an area filled with wonderful shops, superb restaurants, art galleries, and more.

If you aren't lucky or wealthy enough to live in this paradise, La Jolla is a perfect place for a romantic getaway. The shops and restaurants are only a short walk from fine hotels and excellent inns.

The name La Jolla comes from the Spaniards, who called it "La Hoya" (The Cave). The caves can be seen at La Jolla Cove by taking the 133-step stairway down from the La Jolla Cave and Shell Shop (1325 Coast Boulevard). The clear waters of the cove are part of the San Diego-La Jolla Underwater Park, a marine preserve, and are popular with divers and snorkelers.

The point west of the caves is the site of the Ellen Browning Scripps Park, a perfect place for watching the sun set or just relaxing during the day, especially after touring the shops and galleries. The nearby beaches are beautiful and fine for bathers. The strands at La Jolla Cove and at Marine Street Park south of the point are popular bathing places. Children's Pool at the south end of the Scripps Park is a nice beach with shallow waters and gentle surf for the less adventurous.

A block inland from the point and the Shell Shop is Prospect Street, the Champs-Élysées of La Jolla. Here are found the excellent shops and restaurants of the exclusive and chic village. Our favorites include the sculpture and jewelry at the Contemporary Southwest Galleries (7863 Girard Street) and the wildlife art at Black Duck Creek Gallery (7556 Fay Avenue). Other fine boutiques are located on Coast Boulevard and Girard Street.

The La Jolla Museum of Contemporary Art (700 Prospect Street) has an outstanding collection of contemporary art and furnishings. A bit farther away is the Scripps Institute of Oceanography (8602 La Jolla Shore Drive), which has a fine aquarium and also sponsors boat trips to see the whales that migrate off these shores from December to March.

✪ MENDOCINO

Mendocino is a bit of New England transported to the rugged northern coast of California. The village was founded by lumberjacks from Maine in the mid-1800s, and they brought along with them their vision of architecture. The Cape Cod–style homes and buildings would be out of place in much of the state, but on this rugged and wild northern coast, they fit in just fine.

Mendocino has long attracted artists, who found the pounding surf, rugged and rocky shore, and dramatically beautiful redwood country just north inspirational. This legacy of art can be found in the numerous galleries and shops in the village.

These galleries are clustered along Lansing Street between Little Lake Road and the coast, with more showrooms found on Albion and Main streets paralleling the shore.

Our favorites include the crafts at the Ruth Carlson Gallery (Main Street and Highway 1), wearable art at the Great Put-On (corner of Kasten and Main streets), and the collection of creations by local artists at the Artists Co-Op of Mendocino (corner of Main and Osborne streets). Other local artists teach classes and display their creations at the Mendocino Art Center (45200 Little Lake Street).

Other attractions include the lovely historic buildings in town, such as the MacCallum House (45020 Albion Street) and the Mendocino Hotel (45080 Main Street), both gingerbread Victorian homes worth seeing.

In the nearby countryside are other sights, including the Mendocino Headlands State Park, on the coastal bluffs bordering the village, and the Mendocino Coast Botanical Gardens on Highway 1 just north of town. The Gardens has trails to the sea and lookouts that offer great views of the whale migration. The rhododendrons bloom from April to June, with other varieties blooming from May to September. Near the Gardens is Jughandle Creek State Reserve, where you can take a self-guided tour of the wild coast region, or join a ranger-led hike of the creek's environs (call 707/937-5804 for an appointment). Farther inland, the many wineries of Mendocino County beckon (see Chapter Two).

Mendocino has two big annual festivals. The most popular is the Whale Festival, which celebrates the migration of the huge mammals with a festival of art, food, and wine every March. In July, members of the San Francisco Symphony and San Francisco Opera are joined by local musicians in the Mendocino Music Festival. Ten performances are offered over a number of days.

✿ SANTA BARBARA

Santa Barbara is a coastal paradise rich in natural beauty, historical sites, and cultural activities. Settled by the Spanish in 1602,

Santa Barbara cherishes its Spanish heritage, which is evident in its adobe-and-red-tile architecture common in the town.

The Santa Barbara Mission at Laguna and Mission streets is a beautifully preserved church that still holds services. From its location on the eucalyptus-covered hillside, the mission has a commanding view of Santa Barbara, its long, beautiful beach, the Pacific Ocean, and the Channel Islands 11 miles offshore.

In addition, the Spanish heritage is visible at the El Presidio State Historic Park (123 E. Canon Perdido Street). The Presidio was built in 1782 and served as one of four fortresses built along the coast of California. The adobe guardhouse is original and is the oldest building owned by California. The Spanish heritage is celebrated for five days in early August with an Old Spanish Days Fiesta.

Other major attractions in Santa Barbara include the Botanical Gardens (1212 Mission Canyon Road, about 1.5 miles past the mission); the Santa Barbara Orchid Estate (1250 Orchid Drive), a lush display of thousands of orchids, cymbidiums, and other species; the Museum of Natural History (2559 Puesta del Sol Road, a block from the mission); the small but lush Santa Barbara Zoo (500 Ninos Drive); and, just a short walk away, the Andree Clark Bird Refuge (1400 E. Carbillo Boulevard), a serene lagoon and park as popular with joggers as with birdwatchers.

A few blocks south of the Presidio, on Canon Perdido Street between State and Anacapa streets, is El Paseo—a maze of shops and galleries built around one of Santa Barbara's oldest adobe houses. The arcade is meant to resemble that of a plaza in Spain, but the connection is tenuous. The shopping, however, is superb. This is but one of several shopping arcades in downtown Santa Barbara. La Arcada, in the 1100 block of State Street, holds more than a score of shops, boutiques, and restaurants.

In El Paseo and along State Street are Gallery 113, which has paintings and jewelry, and the Elizabeth Fortner Gallery, which has contemporary fine crafts (both at 1114 State Street); the Delphine Gallery (1324 State Street) has paintings of landscapes by local artists; the Nature Trail (931 State Street) has wildlife art; the well-known Chanel and I. Magnin (1415 State Street); and Folks (616 State Street), which has crafts by more than 50 artisans.

Santa Barbara's celebration of art is also visible at the fine Museum of Art (1130 State Street). The permanent collection includes works by Hopper, Monet, Grandma Moses, as well as sculpture and other art from Asia and the Mideast. The Arlington Center for the Performing Arts (1317 State Street) hosts entertainment from Broadway shows to rock concerts.

More art, if you should need it, can be found a half-hour car ride east in the Ojai Valley, which served as the landscape used in the 1936 movie *Lost Horizon*. Ojai, the town, is a sleepy town flanked by mountains. The works of local artists are displayed in the shopping arcade on the main street (Route 150) and every Sunday in the Security Bank parking lot (205 W. Ojai Avenue).

Art can also be found every Sunday in Palm Park, the palm-shaded lawn east of Stearns Wharf on the beach, where local artists display and sell their creations.

The beach here is magnificent. You can swim, sunbathe, or take part in a volleyball game on either end of the shore. The Stearns Wharf is a half-mile long. You can walk out to the shops and restaurants on its far end or drive for a fee (if you don't buy anything during your visit).

In the distance, the five Channel Islands hold promise of adventure. Island Packers offers day and overnight camping trips to three of the islands. What you will see is an unspoiled wilderness that is home to sea lions, numerous species of birds, and tidal pools filled with sea life. From December through March, gray whales migrate in these waters, and the huge mammals offer a fascinating sight. Boat trips to see the whales are offered by the Santa Barbara Museum of Natural History and local outfitters.

Santa Barbara is close to several wineries. The county's oldest, the Santa Barbara Winery, occupies a warehouse (202 Anacapa Street) and offers informal tours and tastings. Other wineries can be found off Highway 101 north of town. The Santa Ynez Valley Winery is on Refugio Road, two miles east of Solvang (a touristy mock re-creation of a Danish village) on Highway 246, and three other winery operations—Vega, Sanford, and Sanford & Benedict—are on Santa Rosa Road west of Buellton. All offer tours and tastings.

Any visit to Santa Barbara should include a drive down the Coast Village Road to Montecito, a very upscale community with more shops and galleries, and a stop at the magnificent Biltmore Hotel. From the restaurant terrace of this Four Seasons hotel, a beautiful mission-style building graced by well-landscaped grounds, you can have a drink and watch the sun go down over the islands in the distance.

As the sun sets, turn away and look inland to the mountains behind this very special village. They slowly turn a lovely shade of purple.

It's a magnificent sight.

✪ FOR MORE INFORMATION

Carmel

Carmel Business Association. San Carlos Street and Seventh Avenue, P.O. Box 4444, Carmel-by-the-Sea, CA 93921. 408/ 624-2522.

Laguna Beach

Laguna Beach Chamber of Commerce. 357 Glenneyre, P.O. Box 396, Laguna Beach, CA 92652. 714/494-1018.

La Jolla

La Jolla Town Council. 1055 Wall Street, Suite 110, P.O. Box 1101, La Jolla, CA 92038. 619/454-1444.

Mendocino

Mendocino County Convention and Visitors Bureau. 320 South State Street, P.O. Box 244, Ukiah, CA 95482. 707/462-3091.

Santa Barbara

Santa Barbara Visitor Information Center. One Santa Barbara Street, P.O. Box 299, Santa Barbara, CA 93102. 805/965-3021.

✪ WHERE AND WHEN

Carmel

Carmel Mission. Rio Road and Lausen Drive. Open Monday to Saturday 8:30 AM to 4:30 PM, Sunday 10:30 AM to 4:30 PM. 408/624-3600.

Carmel River State Park. Off the Scenic Road south of the beach. Open daily. 408/649-2836.

Chateau Julien. From Carmel, 5.1 miles east on Carmel Valley Road. Open 8:30 AM to 5 PM weekdays. 408/624-2600.

Point Lobos State Reserve. On Highway 1, 3 miles south of Carmel. Open 9 AM to 7 PM May through September, 9 AM to 5 PM October through April. 408/624-4909.

Tor House. 26304 Ocean View Road. Open for tours by appointment between 10 AM and 4 PM Friday and Saturday. 408/624-1813.

Laguna Beach

Laguna Art Museum. 307 Cliff Drive. Open 11 AM to 5 PM Tuesday to Sunday. 714/494-6531.

San Juan Capistrano Mission. Ortega Highway and Camino Capistrano in San Juan Capistrano. Open 7:30 AM to 5 PM daily. 714/493-1424.

La Jolla

La Jolla Museum of Contemporary Art. 700 Prospect Street. Open 10 AM to 5 PM Tuesday to Sunday, 10 AM to 9 PM Wednesday. 619/454-3541.

Scripps Aquarium. 8602 La Jolla Shores Drive. Open 9 AM to 5 PM daily. 619/534-6933.

Mendocino

Jughandle Creek Tours. Jughandle State Reserve, on Highway 1 north of town. By appointment. 707/937-5804.

Mendocino Coast Botanical Gardens. 18220 Highway 1, north of town. Open 9 AM to 5 PM daily. 707/965-4352.

Santa Barbara

Andree Clark Bird Refuge. 1400 E. Cabrillo Rd. Open daily. 805/564-5433.

Arlington Center for the Performing Arts. 1317 State Street. Call for performance times. 805/963-4408.

El Presidio State Park. 122 East Canon Perdido Street. Open weekdays from 10:30 AM to 4:30 PM, noon to 4 PM weekends. 805/966-9719.

Sanford and Benedict Vineyards. From Buellton, nine miles west on Santa Rosa Road. Tastings and tours by appointment. 805/688-8314.

Sanford Winery. From Buellton, 4.8 miles south on Santa Rosa Road. Open 11 AM to 4 PM Monday to Saturday. 805/688-3300.

Santa Barbara Botanic Gardens. 1212 Mission Canyon Road. Open daily 8 AM to sunset. Guided tours at 10:30 AM Thursday, 11 AM Sunday. 805/682-4713.

Santa Barbara Museum of Art. 1130 State Street. Open 11 AM to 5 PM Tuesday to Saturday. Tours at 2 PM. 805/963-4364.

Santa Barbara Museum of Natural History. 2559 Puesta del Sol Road. Open 9 AM to 5 PM weekdays, 10 AM to 5 PM weekends. 805/682-4711.

Santa Barbara Orchid Estate. 1250 Orchid Drive. Open 8 AM to 4:30 PM Monday to Saturday, 10 AM to 4 PM Sunday. 805/967-1284.

Santa Barbara Winery. 202 Anacapa Street. Open 9:30 AM to 5 PM daily. 805/963-3633.

Santa Ynez Valley Winery. Two miles east of Solvang on Highway 246, then 1 mile south on Refugio Road. Open 10 AM to 4 PM daily. 805/688-8381.

Santa Barbara Zoo. 500 Ninos Drive. Open 10 AM to 5 PM daily. 805/963-6310.

Stearns Wharf. Where State Street meets the beach. Open daily. 805/963-1979.

Vega Winery. From Buellton, .7 mile south on Santa Rosa Road. Open 10 AM to 4 PM daily. 805/688-2415.

✪ ROMANTIC RETREATS

These five wonderful towns are full of romantic inns and superb restaurants. Here are our favorites, but first an explanation of their breakdown into cost categories.

One night in a hotel, resort, or inn for two:

Inexpensive	Less than $75
Moderate	$75 to $125
Expensive	More than $125

Dinner for two (drinks not included):

Inexpensive	Less than $25
Moderate	$25 to $60
Expensive	More than $60

Carmel: Romantic Lodging

✪ *Carmel Valley Ranch.* Contemporary California meets country in this new resort in the Carmel Valley. The 100 rooms are spacious and furnished with quilts and other country touches. The

The Annual Visit of the Whales

It begins around Thanksgiving in the frigid waters off Alaska. Huge herds of gray whales numbering in the thousands begin their annual migration south to the waters off Baja California in Mexico. The route never varies: east from Alaska, then closer into the California coast near Point Reyes, back out again before returning close to shore off Southern California.

The whales are an awesome sight, rolling and breaking the surface. No matter how many times you have seen them in National Geographic documentaries, experiencing these giant mammals up close is an experience one never forgets. The gray whales are giants. The females, the larger of the sexes, can reach 50 feet in length and weigh up to 45 tons.

The whales' arrival touches off numerous festivals on land to celebrate their passage as well as luring out the whalewatchers by the boatloads. Dana Point Harbor in Orange County holds a Festival of the Whales the last weekend in March (call 714/493-5794) while Mendocino and other north coast communities hold celebrations on several March weekends (call 707/964-3153).

The sightseeing boats sail from December through March. The following lists places to call for a boating expedition to see these marvelous mammals.

Dana Point
  Dana Wharf Sport Fishing (714/496-5794)
  Orange County Marine Institute (714/831-3850)

Fort Bragg
  Anchor Charter Boats (707/964-4550)

Half Moon Bay
  Captain John's (415/728-3377)
  Oceanic Society Expeditions (415/474-3385)

Long Beach
  Queen's Wharf (213/432-8993)

Monterey
  Chris Fishing Trips (408/375-5951)
  Monterey Sport Fishing (408/372-2203)
  Princess Monterey Cruises (408/372-2628)
  Sam's Fishing Fleet (408/372-0577)

Morro Bay
  Virg's Fish'n Inc. (805/772-1223)

Point Reyes
  Point Reyes Field Seminars (415/663-1200)

San Diego
  Biological Adventures (619/222-0391)
  H&M Landing (619/222-1144)
  San Diego Natural History Museum (619/232-3821)

San Francisco
  Oceanic Society Expeditions (415/474-3385)

San Pedro
  Catalina Channel Express (213/519-7971)
  Catalina Cruises (213/253-9800)

Santa Barbara
  Santa Barbara Museum of Natural History
    (805/682-4334)
  Sea Center (805/962-0885)
  Sea Landing Sportfishing (805/963-3564)

Santa Cruz
  Tom's Fishermen's Supply (408/476-2648)

Ventura
  Island Packers (805/642-1393)

California flair comes from the fireplaces, cathedral ceilings, and decks. Expensive. 1 Old Ranch Road, Carmel, CA 93923. 408/625-9500 and 800/4CARMEL.

✪ *Carriage House Inn.* Small (13 rooms) and rustic, this inn offers sunken baths, fireplaces, and spacious rooms. Moderate. Junipero Avenue between Seventh and Eighth avenues, P.O. Box 1900, Carmel, CA 93921. 408/625-2585 and 800/422-4732 in California.

✦ *Cobblestone Inn.* This quaint country inn is built around a courtyard garden and offers 24 rooms, each individually decorated in country pine furniture. Every room has a fireplace. Moderate. Junipero between Seventh and Eighth avenues, P.O. Box 3185, Carmel, CA 93921. 408/625-5222.

✦ *Highlands Inn.* John Steinbeck and Jack London loved it. Tom Selleck, Debra Winger, and Timothy Hutton consider it home. What they found was a 145-room hotel located on a bluff overlooking the Pacific. It has the best view of any inn in Carmel. The rooms are luxurious condo-style, with full kitchens, decks, and fireplaces. Expensive. Four miles south of Carmel on Highway 1, Box 1700, Carmel, CA 93921. 408/624-3801; and 800/682-4811 in California, 800/538-9525 elsewhere in the United States.

✦ *Holiday House.* Surrounded by beautifully landscaped lawns, this brown shingled home offers six guest rooms (four with private baths). The rooms are comfortable and furnished with a mixture of antiques and oddities. Moderate. Camino Real at Seventh Avenue, P.O. Box 782, Carmel, CA 93921. 408/624-6267.

✦ *Quail Lodge.* The 100 luxurious rooms at this elegant five-star resort are located on the grounds of a private country club next to an 800-acre wilderness preserve. The decor is a mix of Oriental and European styles. Expensive. 8205 Valley Greens Drive, Carmel, CA 93923. 408/624-1581; and 800/682-9303 in California, 800/538-9516 elsewhere in the United States.

✦ *Sandpiper Inn.* Simple elegance is the word for this 15-room inn with a view of the beach and sea. There are 13 rooms in the main house, 2 in the back, and all have private baths and antique decor. Expensive. 2408 Bay View Avenue, Carmel, CA 93923. 408/624-6433.

✪ *Stonehouse Inn.* This inn made of stone and glass offers six guest rooms, all named after authors. All rooms share baths. The decor of the rooms is country antiques. The large living room is a popular place for pre-dinner drinks before the fireplace. Moderate. Monte Verde and Eighth streets, P.O. Box 2517, Carmel, CA 93921. 408/624-4569.

✪ *Stonepine.* A former estate of a wealthy banking family, this 330-acre secluded resort now offers 12 luxurious rooms. Eight of the rooms are in the formal main house. These rooms are very elegant and are furnished with antiques. The four other rooms are in the ranch-style annex, and they are luxurious but less stuffy. Facilities include pool and tennis. Expensive. 150 East Carmel Valley Road, Box 1543, Carmel Valley, CA 93924. 408/659-2245.

✪ *Tickle Pink Country Inn.* The 34 rooms are simple but comfortable in this quiet, secluded inn with spectacular views. Expensive. 155 Highland Drive, Carmel, CA 93923. 408/624-1244 and 800/635-4774.

✪ *Valley Lodge.* The cottages on this secluded country retreat offer 31 rooms, all furnished with antiques and fireplaces. The cottages are surrounded by 3 acres of gardens. Facilities include a pool and hot tub. Expensive. 8 Ford Road, P.O. Box 93, Carmel Valley, 93924. 408/659-2261 and 800/641-4646.

Carmel: Fine Dining

✪ *La Boheme.* The menu is fixed—three courses: salad, soup, and one entree—but this French restaurant can be excellent. Moderate. Seventh Avenue and Dolores Street. 408/624-7500.

✪ *The Covey at Quail Lodge.* Fine continental cuisine served in a lovely room next to a romantic lake. Expensive. 8205 Valley Greens Drive. 408/624-1581.

✪ *Crème Carmel.* Californian cuisine with a French touch at this bright small dining room. Moderate. San Carlos Street near Seventh Avenue. 408/624-0444.

✪ *L'Escargot.* Cozy room decorated with antiques and flowers, fine French cuisine where the chef's specials really are special. Expensive. Mission Street and Fourth Avenue. 408/624-4914.

✪ *Gold Fork.* Excellent and creative continental cuisine. Don't overlook the weekly game specials. Moderate. Ocean Avenue between Third Avenue and Dolores Street. 408/624-2569.

✪ *Hog's Breath Inn.* The name is certainly unusual, but Clint Eastwood can call his restaurant anything he wants. The menu is basic meat and seafood and the atmosphere is like that of a pub. Moderate. San Carlos Street and Fifth Avenue. 408/625-1044.

✪ *Pacific's Edge.* The dramatic views of the coast enhance the innovative Californian cuisine. Entertainment and dancing Friday and Saturday. Expensive. Highway 1. 408/624-3801.

✪ *Rio Grill.* Santa Fe–style meat and seafood dishes are the stars at this casual spot with southwestern adobe decor. Moderate. Crossroads Shopping Center at Highway 1 and Rio Road. 408/625-5436.

Laguna Beach: Romantic Lodging

✪ *Blue Lantern Inn.* There are 29 modern rooms with wonderful views of the harbor at this new, Cape Cod–style inn on the waterfront in Dana Point, south of Laguna Beach. The rooms have jacuzzis and fireplaces. Expensive. 34343 Street of the Blue Lantern, Dana Point, CA 92629. 714/661-1304.

❂ *Carriage House.* There are six comfortable suites in this inn that's surrounded by a beautiful garden. Expensive. 1322 Catalina Street, Laguna Beach, CA 92651. 714/494-8945.

❂ *Dana Point Resort.* Casual yet elegant, this lovely new resort offers 350 rooms, all very spacious and tastefully decorated. Facilities include two pools, three spas, and a health club. Expensive. 25135 Park Lantern Avenue, Dana Point, CA 92629. 714/661-5000.

❂ *Eiler's Inn.* This comfortable 12-room inn was named after Eiler Larson, a Danish immigrant who was the official greeter of the town from the 1960s until his death in 1975. Built around a lovely courtyard, the rooms have private baths and a 1940s Californian decor. Ask for the large upstairs room with the fireplace. Moderate. 741 South Coast Highway, Laguna Beach, CA 92651. 714/494-3004.

❂ *Ritz-Carlton.* The gathering spot for Orange County and California's wealthy and important, this five-star resort is one of the finest hotels in the nation. The grounds are beautifully landscaped and are home to families of rabbits and an assortment of birds including hummingbirds. The views of the beach and ocean from the blufftop location are magnificent, and surpassed only by the sunsets. The lobby and other public areas are luxurious, the service is impeccable and the 393 guest rooms are wonderful. Facilities include three restaurants, two pools, beach, health club, and golf course. Expensive. 33533 Ritz Carlton Drive, Laguna Niguel, CA 92677. 714/240-2000.

Laguna Beach: Fine Dining

✪ *Las Brisas.* Nouvelle Mexican and killer margaritas at this popular spot. Moderate. 361 Cliff Drive, Laguna Beach. 714/497-5434.

✪ *Cafe Zoolu.* Trendy, artsy, and in, featuring the latest in cuisines. Call for this week's style. Moderate. 860 Glenneyre, Laguna Beach. 714/494-6825.

✪ *Cedar Creek Inn.* Pastas and seafood, with entertainment. Moderate. 384 Forest Avenue, Laguna Beach. 714/497-8696.

✪ *Five Feet Restaurant.* Excellent Chinese dishes served in a very sophisticated environment. Moderate. 328 Glenneyre, Laguna Beach. 714/497-4955.

✪ *Kachine.* Wonderful Southwestern fare in a chic cafe. Moderate. 222 Forest Avenue, Laguna Beach. 714/497-5546.

✪ *Mezzaluna.* Fine Italian cuisine served in very chic surroundings. Expensive. 2441 East Coast Highway, Corona Del Mar. 714/675-2004.

✪ *Renaissance Cafe.* Specialty coffees, live music, and light fare make this an attractive place for a break from shopping. Inexpensive. 234 Forest Avenue, Laguna Beach. 714/497-JAVA.

✪ *Ritz-Carlton.* The Dining Room is elegant and formal, and the nouvelle cuisine is fine, yet not quite as perfect as the setting. The Cafe, however, offers a more casual and creative menu featuring nouvelle Californian cuisine as well as some Mexican dishes. It is sensational. The Sunday brunch in the Cafe is fantastic. Expensive. 33533 Ritz Carlton Drive, Laguna Niguel. 714/240-2000.

✿ *Ruby's Diner.* It's for fun, but this re-creation of a 1950s diner comes complete with the music, the cars-as-period-sculpture, and the decor. The food is okay, but it's the mood that counts. Try it for breakfast or lunch. Inexpensive. 30622 South Coast Highway, Laguna Beach. 714/497-RUBY.

✿ *Wahoo's Fish Taco.* Californian cuisine with an emphasis on health-conscious cooking and fresh seafood. Moderate. 1133 South Coast Highway, Laguna Beach. 714/497-0033.

La Jolla: Romantic Lodging

✿ *The Bed and Breakfast Inn at La Jolla.* Built in 1913 (John Philip Sousa lived here in the 1920s), this lovely inn is a stunning example of Cubist architecture. The 16 guest rooms are charming and furnished in "cottage" style. Ten of the rooms are in the main house; the rest are in the annex. Many of the rooms have fireplaces and ocean views. Some of the best rooms are the Holiday Room, with a four-poster canopied bed, antique armoire, and white and cream color scheme, the feminine Ocean Breeze Room and its decor of flowers with a touch of country French, and the Pacific View Room, an antique-filled room that has a nautical air. Moderate. 7753 Draper Avenue, La Jolla, CA 92037. 619/456-2066.

✿ *Colonial Inn.* Old-world elegance and style in a restored Victorian house in the center of town. There are 75 rooms, and some are small. Expensive. 910 Prospect Street, La Jolla, CA 92307. 619/454-2181 and 800/832-5525 nationwide.

✿ *Prospect Park Inn.* This contemporary 25-room inn in the heart of La Jolla's shopping district offers stunning views of the ocean from its back rooms. The decor is contemporary Californian casual. If a view is desired, ask for the View rooms. Moderate/

expensive. 1110 Prospect Street, La Jolla, CA 92037. 619/454-0133; and 800/345-8577 in California, 800/433-1609 elsewhere in the United States.

❂ *Torrey Pines Inn.* This 75-room hotel located on an oceanfront bluff 10 minutes north of La Jolla offers spacious and luxurious rooms as well as a serene setting. Moderate. 11480 Torrey Pines Road, La Jolla, CA 92037. 619/453-4420.

❂ *La Valencia.* There are 100 rooms in this lovely hotel, which has a garden terrace for drinks and light dining, an exercise room, and lawn games. The rooms are comfortable and tastefully decorated. Expensive. 1132 Prospect Street, La Jolla, CA 92037. 619/454-0771 and 800/451-0772 nationwide.

❂ *Westbourne Windansea Bed and Breakfast.* This charming inn offers three cute and cozy rooms, each individually furnished. One room has antique furniture, another has oriental furnishings, and the third has lacquered pieces. Moderate. 537 Westbourne Street, La Jolla, CA 92037. 619/456-9634.

La Jolla: Fine Dining

❂ *Cindy Black's.* Classic French cuisine, featuring seafood and lamb in a beautiful restaurant decorated with original art. Moderate. 5721 La Jolla Boulevard. 619/456-6299.

❂ *El Crab Catcher.* Dine outdoors on the patio and watch the cove at this excellent (but casual) seafood restaurant. Moderate. 1298 Prospect Street in the Coast Walk Mall. 619/454-9587.

❂ *George's at the Cove.* The seafood is grand at this lovely, art-filled room. Try the small terrace with beautiful views of the cove and the Pacific. Expensive. 1250 Prospect Street in the Prospect Place Mall. 619/454-4244.

✪ *Issimo.* Small but superb, this fine Italian restaurant serves wonderfully delicious pastas and veal dishes. Expensive. 5634 La Jolla Boulevard. 619/454-7004.

✪ *St. James Bar.* Fine French cuisine, but choose the seafood. The setting is beautiful, too, with marble, artworks and antiques completing a perfect picture. Expensive. 4370 La Jolla Village Drive. 619/453-6650.

✪ *La Valencia Hotel.* In nice weather, have a drink in the garden courtyard outside this absolutely lovely pink hotel and then move inside to either the Sky Room (fine French food and excellent views of the ocean), or the Whaling Bar Dining Room (seafood and meats). Expensive. 1132 Prospect Street. 619/454-0771.

Mendocino: Romantic Lodging

✪ *Albion River Inn.* The location—a cliff overlooking the sea—is stunning and is matched by the antique-filled decor in this inn's 20 rooms. Moderate/expensive. Six miles south of Mendocino on Highway 1. Albion, CA 95410. 707/937-1919.

✪ *Glendeven.* The 12 rooms (8 in the main house, 4 in the annex) are charming, filled with a mixture of country furniture and whimsical art. Moderate. 8221 North Highway 1, Little River, CA 95456. 707/937-0083.

✪ *Headlands Inn.* It was a barbershop, a saloon, a hotel annex, and then a private home. And then it was moved to its present site. This three-story Victorian offers five guest rooms (four in the house, one in an adjacent cottage), all with fireplaces and antique furnishings and either a garden or ocean view. Breakfast is exceptional. Moderate. P.O. Box 132, Mendocino, CA 95460. 707/937-4431.

✿ *Howard Creek Ranch.* There are three rooms (two share a bath) in this New England–style house on a small ranch in a secluded valley east of Mendocino. There are also two additional rooms in a converted boat and a rustic cabin. The rooms are furnished with country pieces. Ask for a room in the main house. Moderate. Highway 1, 3 miles north of Westport. P.O. Box 121, Westport, CA 95488. 707/964-6725.

✿ *Joshua Grindle Inn.* This inn would be at home on the coast of Maine. It's surrounded by a white picket fence, the furniture is Early American and the quilts were handmade in New England. There are five guest rooms in the house, three in a new water-tower-like structure and two in a cottage in the back. Moderate. 44800 Little Lake Road, P.O. Box 647, Mendocino, CA 95460. 707/937-4143.

✿ *MacCallum House.* Considered the finest Victorian house in Mendocino, this inn offers 12 rooms in the main house and nine more in cottages around a garden. All the rooms are decorated with Victorian period furnishings. Moderate/expensive. 45020 Albion Street, P.O. Box 206, Mendocino, CA 95460. 707/937-0289.

✿ *1021 Main Street.* Unusual, to say the least. This four-room (two in the main house, two in the cottages called the Foundry and the Zen House) inn offers privacy, fantastic views of the ocean, and unusual objets d'art. Moderate. 1021 Main Street, Mendocino, CA 95460. 707/937-5150.

✿ *Mendocino Farmhouse.* White picket fence, gardens of sweet william, candytufts, and other delicate flowers, and a two-story farmhouse make this three-room inn a special find. Inexpensive. Olson Lane, off the Comptche-Ukiah Road east of Mendocino. P.O. Box 247, Mendocino, CA 95460. 707/937-0241.

✪ *Mendocino Village Inn.* The 12 guest rooms in this Queen Anne Victorian inn are furnished in an eclectic mix. Ten of the rooms have private baths (two share a bath), seven have fireplaces, and several have private entrances. Each room has a different decor, ranging from Indian (the Quilt Room) to Victorian (the Diamond Lil Room) to nautical (Captain's Quarters). Moderate. 44860 Main Street, P.O. Box 626, Mendocino, CA 95460. 707/937-0246.

✪ *Stanford Inn by the Sea.* Facing the Pacific and overlooking Mendocino, this rustic inn has the feel of a mountain lodge despite an abundance of luxury. The 25 rooms have wood walls and ceilings, wood-burning stoves and fireplaces, country furnishings including four-poster beds, and floral prints. Each room has a balcony or patio. A Cape Cod–style cottage offers two bedrooms, a full kitchen, and a living room. Moderate/expensive. Southeast of Mendocino on the Comptche-Ukiah Road. P.O. Box 487, Mendocino, CA 95460. 707/937-5615.

✪ *Whitegate Inn.* The five guest rooms in this elegant inn have fireplaces and are furnished with antiques and decorated with lace curtains and other tasteful fabrics. The gazebo on the lawn is popular for weddings. Moderate. 499 Howard Street, P.O. Box 150, Mendocino, CA 95460. 707/937-4892.

Mendocino: Fine Dining

✪ *Albion River Inn.* Continental fare featuring seafood and pasta at this lovely bed-and-breakfast. Expensive. 3790 North Highway 1, Albion. 707/937-1919.

✪ *Cafe Beaujolais.* Superb (and calorie-laden) country cooking at this rustic spot. Breakfast and lunch daily, dinner Thursday through Sunday. Moderate. 961 Ukiah Street. 707/937-5614.

❂ *MacCallum House.* Fine continental dining in a very charming Victorian bed-and-breakfast. Moderate. 45020 Albion Street. 707/937-5763.

❂ *955 Ukiah Street Restaurant.* Californian cuisine—fresh vegetables, pastas, and the like—served up with flair. Moderate. 955 Ukiah Street. 707/937-1955.

❂ *Sea Gull.* Popular with locals, this casual restaurant serves excellent omelets as well as fish and meat dishes. Moderate. Lansing and Ukiah streets. 707/937-2100.

Santa Barbara: Romantic Lodging

❂ *Bath Street Inn.* There are seven antique-filled guest rooms in this lovely three-story Queen Anne Victorian inn. All rooms have private baths. Moderate. 1720 Bath Street, Santa Barbara, CA 93101. 805/682-9680.

❂ *Bayberry Inn.* The eight rooms in this 1886 Federal-style inn are decorated with antiques, canopied beds, and beautiful fabrics. Expensive. 111 West Valerio Street, Santa Barbara, CA 93101. 805/682-3199.

❂ *Cheshire Cat.* Two white-and-beige Victorian houses make up this striking inn, which offers 11 rooms, carefully decorated in Laura Ashley fabrics and colors. Moderate/expensive. 36 West Valerio Street, Santa Barbara, CA 93101. 805/569-1610.

❂ *Four Seasons Biltmore.* Glorious, beautiful, romantic—this 236-room inn has it all. The hotel is built on the former estate of a copper baron. The rooms, all spacious and nicely furnished (the suites have fireplaces), are located in low stucco and red-tile-roof buildings spread around the perfectly landscaped lawns and gardens. Wood beams, wooden shutters, tiled entryways, and other touches make this hotel a very special and very romantic retreat. Amenities include two pools (including an Olympic-sized heated pool at the large and chic Coral Casino Club on the beach), tennis, and golf. Expensive. 1260 Channel Drive, Santa Barbara, CA 93108. 805/969-2261 and 800/332-3442 nationwide.

☉ *Glenborough Inn.* There are nine guest rooms in this inn, but the place to stay is its annex in the century-old cottage across the street. The four rooms in the cottage have private baths (only one room of the five in the main house has a private bath), separate entrances, and a garden. Decor in all the rooms is a mixture of antiques and wicker. Moderate. 1327 Bath Street, Santa Barbara, CA 93101. 805/966-0589.

☉ *Inn at Summer Hill.* Ocean views, fireplaces, jacuzzis, and antiques make this 16-room inn on the coast east of Santa Barbara a stunning retreat. Expensive. 2520 Lillie Avenue, Summerland, CA 93067. 805/969-9998 and 800/999-8999 nationwide.

☉ *Ojai Manor Hotel.* Simple elegance blending turn-of-the-century furnishings with contemporary works of art make this six-room hotel in Ojai a lovely retreat. Inexpensive. 210 East Matilija, Ojai, CA 93023. 805/646-0961.

☉ *Ojai Valley Inn and Country Club.* Recently renovated, this mission-style resort offers 218 luxurious rooms. The facilities are stylish and extensive, offering lushly landscaped grounds, golf, tennis, two pools, saunas, and steam rooms. Expensive. Country Club Road, Ojai, CA 93023. 805/646-5511 and 800/422-OJAI nationwide.

☉ *Old Yacht Club Inn.* This historic structure once faced the ocean on Cabrillo Boulevard and served as the headquarters of the local yacht club. Later moved to its present location, this inn now offers five rooms in the main house and four more in the adjacent Hitchcock House. All rooms have private baths, colorful print decor, and antique furnishings. The nicest rooms are those at the front, for they get a breeze and sun. Moderate. 431 Corona Del Mar Drive, Santa Barbara, CA 93103. 805/962-1277.

☻ *The Parsonage.* This century-old Queen Anne Victorian inn is lovely, and its six guest rooms, all furnished with a mix of antiques and kitsch personal pieces, are no less attractive. The finest room is the Honeymoon Suite, which stretches across the front of the house and offers striking views of the ocean. Moderate. 1600 Olive Street, Santa Barbara, CA 93101. 805/962-9336.

☻ *San Ysidro Ranch.* Popular with Hollywood names, this secluded luxury ranch has 43 rooms set in cottages spread around 14 acres of gardens and orange trees. The rooms are luxurious and the style is very casual, except at dinner, when things become formal. Amenities include a pool, tennis courts, horseback riding, and golf nearby. Expensive. 900 San Ysidro Lane, Montecito, CA 93108. 805/969-5046.

☻ *Sheraton Santa Barbara Hotel & Spa.* The Mediterranean-style decor and the oceanfront location make this 174-room resort a special place. Facilities include the beach across the street, pool, and exercise equipment. Expensive. 1111 East Cabrillo Boulevard, Santa Barbara, CA 93103. 805/963-0744 and 800/325-3535 nationwide.

☻ *Simpson House Inn.* Antiques and original art furnish the six rooms in this 1874 Italianate inn located on 1 acre of beautiful gardens. Four guest rooms have private baths. Expensive. 121 East Arrellaga, Santa Barbara, CA 93101. 805/963-7067.

❂ *Tiffany Inn.* This turn-of-the-century Victorian has seven beautifully decorated rooms, all with four-poster queen-size beds, lovely fabrics, and antiques. Five of the rooms have private baths. Moderate/expensive. 1323 De la Vina Street, Santa Barbara, CA 93101. 805/963-2283.

❂ *Upham Victorian Hotel and Garden Cottages.* The 49 rooms in this 1871 masterpiece hotel and its adjacent garden cottages and carriage house are furnished with antiques and decorated with lovely fabrics. All the rooms have private baths. Expensive. 1404 De la Vina Street, Santa Barbara, CA 93101. 805/962-0058 and 800/727-0876 nationwide.

Santa Barbara: Fine Dining

❂ *Cold Spring Tavern.* More than a century ago, this cozy lodge was a stagecoach stop. Today, the colorful tavern offers fine regional fare. Moderate. 5995 Stagecoach Road, Ojai. 805/ 967-0066.

❂ *Downey's.* Nouvelle Californian cuisine, featuring seafood as well as outstanding lamb and duck. Expensive. 1305 State Street. 805/966-5006.

❂ *El Encanto.* Perhaps the most romantic dining room in the area, the views of the Pacific almost overshadow the fine French and Italian seafood and pasta. Expensive. 1900 Lasuen Road. 805/687-5000.

❂ *The Epicurean.* This elegant and romantic dining room serves fine steaks, seafood, and chicken dishes. Expensive. 125 East Carrillo Street. 805/966-4789.

❂ *Four Seasons Biltmore.* La Marina serves fine continental cuisine while the Patio offers wonderful lunches and the best brunch around on weekends as well as sensational ocean views. Moderate/expensive. 1260 Channel Drive. 805/969-2261.

✪ *Harbor Restaurant.* Simple but fine seafood in a setting on Stearns Wharf where an ocean view is in every direction. Splendid view of the sunsets. Moderate. 210 Stearns Wharf. 805/963-3311.

✪ *Michael's Waterside.* Elegant Californian cuisine, but stick with the seafood dishes. Expensive. 50 Los Patos Way. 805/969-0307.

✪ *Mousse Odile.* Superb French cuisine served in a casual atmosphere. Moderate. 18 East Cota Street. 805/962-5393.

✪ *Palace Cafe.* Funky and casual, this lively cafe serves up fine Cajun and Creole dishes. Moderate. 8 East Cota Street. 805/966-3133.

✪ *Paradise Cafe.* Casual atmosphere of the 1940s, cuisine of today's California featuring grilled meats and seafood. Moderate. 702 Anacapa Street. 805/962-4416.

✪ *La Playa Azul Cafe.* Mexican cuisine served with Californian style and touches. Moderate. 914 Santa Barbara Street. 805/966-2860.

✪ *Ristorante Piatti.* Grilled fish, chicken, and homemade pastas make this modern trattoria a hit. Don't miss the pizzas. Moderate. 516 San Ysidro Road, Montecito. 805/969-7520.

✪ *The Stonehouse.* This restaurant, part of the San Ysidro Ranch, offers excellent California-French cuisine. Moderate. 900 San Ysidro Lane. 805/969-5046.

For more information on other attractions, lodging, and restaurants on the coast around Carmel, Mendocino, and Santa Barbara, see Chapter Three. For information about the wineries around Mendocino, see Chapter Two.

Chapter Two

Wine Country

The Franciscan monks were the first California wine-makers. In 1780, they planted cuttings of European grapes next to their newly founded missions. Now little more than two centuries later, there are more than 300 wineries in the state, most of them in Napa Valley and Sonoma County, the fertile region north of San Francisco Bay where warm days and cool nights provide the perfect setting for grape growing.

These two viticultural regions—Napa and Sonoma—are wonderful places to wander for a day or a week. The lovely vineyards, the golden hills, and the balmy climate are just part of the attraction. Here you will find Spanish missions, the residence of the last Mexican governor of the state, spa towns built around thermal and mud baths, lavish Victorian mansions, elegant resorts and inns, and numerous gourmet restaurants.

Touring this region is best done at a slow pace. You cannot possibly visit all the wineries in one trip. And as for tasting—well, a few tasting stops are enjoyable in a short trip, more than that is a perfect excuse for an overnight stay in one of the many lovely inns.

Mendocino, Napa, and Sonoma are the most interesting of California's wine-making regions. These regions have been broken into three drives: Mendocino County: Highway 101 from Cloverdale to Redwood Valley and Route 128 from Highway 101 to Navarro; Napa: Highway 29 between Napa and Calistoga; and Sonoma: Highway 12 from Sonoma to Santa Rosa and Highway 101 from Santa Rosa to Cloverdale. Major attractions and the wineries we enjoyed visiting are described, but only use our list as a guide; stop at any winery that piques your interest, for by no means is our sampling a comprehensive list of the hundreds of wineries in the region.

What most of these wineries offer is a tour of the winery with an explanation of how the wines are made. The tours often end at a tasting room that usually doubles as a sales room for the winery.

The California wineries produce a wide variety of different wines, ranging from the popular white and red varietals—chardonnay, sauvignon blanc, cabernet sauvignon, and zinfandel—as well as the generics—chablis, sauterne, burgundy, and claret. Some of the wineries also produce sparkling wines—champagnes and sparkling burgundy.

Of the three regions, Napa has the most wineries, the best inns, and the finest restaurants. It's the upscale region, the one where you expect fine crystal, white linens, and fresh flowers on your dinner table. It's also the region where Highway 101 is jammed with cars on some autumn weekends when the harvest is underway. For fewer crowds, a slower pace, and a more casual atmosphere, visit Sonoma and Mendocino counties. Wherever you go, pack a picnic basket. Many of the wineries have picnicking areas, and you can pick up the wine and cheese along the way.

✪ The Sonoma Valley is graced by more than 30 vineyards like this one. (Steve Poffenberger, courtesy of the Sonoma Valley Visitors Bureau)

The best time to visit depends on what you want to see. In the winter, the pace at the wineries is slower, and the winemakers may have more time to describe their art. In the spring and summer, the wine country is a popular weekend destination, with visitors attracted by numerous festivals as much as by the wineries. The busiest time of year is in the last three weeks of September and the first three weeks of August, when the grapes ripen and the harvest gets underway.

The major wine country festivals are the Mendocino Coast Food and Winefest in May, the Russian River Wine Fest in Healdsburg also in May, the Napa Valley Wine Auction in St. Helena in June, and the Valley of the Moon Vintage Festival in Sonoma the last weekend in September.

The wineries we list are open for tours (see the hours and days in the Where and When section). Some wineries charge a small fee for tastings, but they offer hors d'oeuvres to visitors. You can buy wines at the wineries, but do not expect great bargains. The prices are about the same as those in the stores.

✿ MENDOCINO COUNTY

The valleys are narrower, the mountains higher and more rugged, and the wineries newer in Mendocino County. Despite their comparative lack of age, the wineries in Mendocino are beginning to make their vintages known beyond California.

Begin your tour on Highway 101 in the small town of Hopland. Turn north on Uva Road then west to Bel Abres Road and Fetzer Vineyards, which is located in the former Hopland High School. The auditorium is used for wine tastings, and some of the classrooms now serve as shops for crafts, gifts, and other items.

The next stop in this valley is McDowell Valley Vineyards, on

Highway 175, 3.8 miles east of Highway 101. You can tell this is a high-tech operation by the huge array of solar cells and earthworks that help create and conserve energy at the winery.

The tasting room is large and lovely, mixing oak and redwood carved into art deco shapes. Entertainment is provided by a baby grand piano, and dances are sometimes held on the spacious floor.

Continue north on Highway 101 past Ukiah to North State Street and then drive to Parducci Wine Cellars. This winery was founded in 1931 and is the oldest in the county.

There are other wineries on or just off Highway 101 in this valley, but perhaps it's time to double back on Highway 101 past Ukiah to Route 253 and take this scenic mountain road to the Anderson Valley and Highway 128. Drive north on Highway 128 past Philo. There you will find Edmeades Vineyards, Navarro Vineyards, the Lazy Creek Winery, Husch Vineyards, Pepperwood Springs Winery, and the Handley Cellars.

All of these operations are on Highway 128. The oldest winery in this region dates back to only 1971, and most remain small and family owned. Far less well known than those in Napa or Sonoma, a visit to these small wineries is more personal and very pleasant.

✪ NAPA VALLEY

Less than an hour's drive north of San Francisco Bay is the town of Napa, a lovely little community with numerous majestic Victorian Gothic homes and buildings. Napa is the gateway to this fertile wine region, and Highway 29 is the main road to the more than 30,000 acres of vineyards here. The wineries start north of town, in the elegant community of Yountville.

The first stop on our tour is Domaine Chandon, on the California Drive exit west off Highway 29 on the south side of Yountville.

Domaine Chandon is the producer of sparkling wines called *methode champenoise* (they cannot be called champagne for the only true champagnes are from the Champagne province in France). These modern facilities are owned by Moet-Hennessy and Luis Vuitton.

On Highway 29 in Yountville is Vintage 1870, a former converted and expanded into a 22-acre sprawl of boutiques, restaurants, and shops. In Yountville, take the Yountville Cross Road east to Silverado Trail and turn right. This takes you past Silverado Vineyards (owned in part by Lillian Disney, widow of Walt); Stag's Leap Wine Cellars, producers of an internationally acclaimed cabernet sauvignon, and Clos du Val Wine Company, where Bernard Portet, a Frenchman, has created a wonderful cabernet sauvignon.

Take time to visit and sample the wines, if you wish, before returning to Highway 29 and continuing to the north side of Oakville to the Robert Mondavi Winery. The winery looks like an old mission, with white adobe walls and a red tile roof. It was actually built in 1966 and expanded later. The grassy area behind the two wings of the winery is the site of summer art exhibits and concerts.

Another well-known winery is Inglenook-Napa Valley, whose driveway is off Highway 29 just south of Rutherford, the first town north of Oakville. This massive stone winery was built in 1880 by a fur trader and sea captain.

More wineries line Highway 29 between Rutherford and St. Helena, where you will find Beringer, Charles Krug, Christian Brothers/Greystone Cellars, and other famous vintages.

Beringer is on the north side of St. Helena and its winery is behind the ornate Rhine House, which was built by Frederick Beringer in 1876 as a copy of the house he and his brother Jacob left behind in Germany. Tours of the magnificently furnished and decorated mansion end at the winery's tasting room.

On Highway 29 on the north side of town is Charles Krug

Winery, which is inside buildings of stone topped by red roofs and shaded by tall oaks. The buildings were erected in 1861. On the other side of Highway 29 is the huge, century-old stone building that is the home of Christian Brothers/Greystone Cellars. You can take a tour and see Brother Timothy's endless corkscrew collection.

Continue north on Highway 29 to Larkmead Lane and turn right to Hans Kornell Champagne Cellars. Kornell, a refugee of Nazi Germany, started his winery in 1952 in a two-story stone building that was once Larkmead Winery.

A half mile north of Larkmead Lane, turn west on Petersen Lane and then drive to Schramsberg Vineyards, which has been mentioned in several of Robert Louis Stevenson's stories. The current operation is the third reincarnation of the winery the writer visited in 1880.

Continue north on Highway 29 and turn right on Dunaweal Lane, which leads to Sterling Vineyards, in the rambling white structure that resembles the Greek seashore resort of Mykonos. You may take an aerial tramway up to the hilltop winery (round-trip, $3.50).

By now you have reached Calistoga, a thermal-springs resort town named by combining California and Saratoga by a nineteenth-century promoter.

The town isn't big, about six blocks long, and there aren't any buildings more than two stories tall. The attraction, though, isn't the town; it's the thermal springs and some unusual attractions just outside of the village.

A mile north of Calistoga is California's Old Faithful, a geyser that erupts in a plume of 350-degree steam and water 60 feet into the air every 40 minutes. Another natural wonder is the Petrified Forest, on Petrified Forest Road off Highway 128. The forest was created when Mount St. Helena (don't confuse it with Washington State's Mount St. Helens) erupted six million years ago and covered the redwoods and other trees with a layer of ash. In time a chemical process petrified the trees. The forest isn't huge, but there are scores of interesting specimens and a museum to see.

One way to take away the aches from a long drive is by soaking them away in thermal waters. In Calistoga, take a break and soothe those tired muscles at Calistoga Spa Hot Springs, 1006 Washington Street (707/942-6269); Dr. Wilkinson's Hot Springs, 1507 Lincoln Avenue (707/942-4102); Golden Haven Hot Springs Spa, 1713 Lake Street (707/942-6793); or Lincoln Avenue Spa, 1339 Lincoln Avenue (707/942-5296).

✪ SONOMA COUNTY

Sonoma's heritage is a cross section of the early years of California's history. In the Sonoma County Historic Park you can see the Mission San Francisco Solano and its large plaza of historic adobe houses, each a testament to Spain's early colonization in this part of the continent.

After Spain came Mexico, which governed California from Casa Grande, the adobe home of the last Mexican governor, General Mariano Vallejo. Only the servant's wing of Casa Grande remains; a fire destroyed the rest in 1867. The Sonoma Barracks, which is still standing, housed Vallejo's troops.

After Mexican control of California was ended by Americans in 1846, Vallejo moved to his 44,000-acre estate and built a huge Victorian-Gothic house that he called *Lachryma Montis* (Latin for Mountain Tear). The house, now open for tours, is surrounded by gardens and is beautifully decorated with lace curtains, white marble fireplaces, and imported antiques.

The early Spanish presence was crucial to Sonoma's becoming a grape-growing region. The Franciscan missionaries planted vineyards next to the mission in the 1830s, laying the foundation for what was to follow along highways 12 and 101.

Start a tour of Sonoma County south of the town at the

champagne caves of Gloria Ferrer. The Ferrers are a Spanish family that have been making wine for more than 700 years. This winery is named after the wife of the president. It is on Highway 121 1.4 miles south of the junction with Highway 12. The winery's architecture has the flavor of Spain—red tile roof and white stucco walls. Tastings are accompanied by *tapas*.

In Sonoma, not far from the historic area, is Sebastiani Vineyards at 389 Fourth Street E. Their first wine—a zinfandel—was made here in 1895.

Four miles north of town, on Madrone Road, is the Valley of the Moon Winery, whose vineyards were first planted in the 1850s.

Another historic vineyard can be found at Glen Ellen Winery, .8 mile south of Glen Ellen on London Ranch Road. The vines were planted in 1860 by the Wegner family, among the early pioneers in the 1860s. In the hills above the winery is Jack London State Park, which includes the writer's ranch, his burial site, and an interesting museum displaying many of his personal effects.

The final stop before heading on to Santa Rosa and the Russian River Valley is Chateau St. Jean (pronounced as in blue jeans), on Highway 12 just north of the village of Kenwood. The winery, built in the mid-1960s, is distinguished by a mock medieval tower that offers a bird's-eye view of the winery operations. The tasting room and offices are in an old country mansion that dates back to the 1920s.

From this point continue driving northwest to Santa Rosa and Highway 101. The wineries here are often tucked away on small country roads and are not as visible as those in the Napa Valley.

When you reach Highway 101, turn north and continue to the River Road exit then drive 14 miles west to F. Korbel and Bros. This winery has been making sparkling wines since 1882. Tours start in a majestic former railroad depot and end in the tasting room in an elegant stone brandy-barrel warehouse. You may also visit Korbel's lovely rose gardens.

Ride the Rails Through Wine Country

Return to the elegance of a bygone age by taking the Napa Valley Wine Train on a 36-mile roundtrip tour of the wine country between Napa and St. Helena.

Passengers can enjoy the luxury of traveling in refurbished 1915-vintage Pullman Parlor cars drawn by diesel locomotives from the 1950s. The Wine Train operates luncheon excursions every day and dinner trips Tuesdays through Sundays. Brunch trains operate on weekends only.

While viewing the lovely wine country landscape, passengers are served either a delightful three-course lunch featuring entrees such as a filet mignon marinated in red wine and fresh herbs or breast of chicken marinated in white wine and served with chardonnay and tarragon sauce. For the four-course dinner, the options include a filet of Pacific salmon poached in court bouillion with lobster sauce or a mixed grill—rack of lamb, filet mignon, and quail—with pancetta, rosemary, and sauce chasseur. Lunch is $25 and $29 for the train ride; dinner is $45 and $14.50 for the train ride; brunch is $22 and $29 for the train ride. The lunch and dinner costs do not include wine, but the brunch includes champagne. The prices are subject to change.

Once a month, the Wine Train offers a Winemakers Dinner that features a famous Napa Valley winemaker and a special dinner designed to compliment the featured wines. The dinner includes a discussion with the winemaker.

Trains depart from the main depot (1275 McKingstry Street, Napa). Call 707/253-2111 and 800/522-4142 nationwide.

If you turn right on Old Redwood Road, then left on Pleasant Avenue, and left again on Chalk Hill Road, you will come to a country lane lined by eight different wineries. Chalk Hill, Estate William Baccala, Johnson's Alexander Valley (the cellar doubles as a concert hall), and Sausal are just a few of the wineries on the lane. You can take this road and return to Highway 101 by turning left on the Valley Road just past the Sausal Winery, and following Alexander and West Healdsburg avenues to Healdsburg.

If you choose not to take this side road, continue north on Highway 101 to another popular sparkling-wine producer. Piper Sonoma is not only a winery, it's a cultural center. The modern concrete-and-glass winery has a 150-seat theater, an art gallery, and chic tasting salon. Take the Windsor exit west to Old Redwood Highway and then drive north 3 miles to the winery.

The next town north is Healdsburg and the Clos Du Bois, a modern winery operation in a residential neighborhood at 5 Fitch Street, just off Highway 101 in town. If you like high-tech tinker-toys, you'll love this place that is crammed with giant stainless steel tanks and computers controlling every stage of fermentation.

✿ FOR MORE INFORMATION

Mendocino County

Mendocino County Visitors Bureau. 320 South State Street, P.O. Box 244, Ukiah, CA 95482. 707/462-3091.

Napa Valley

Napa Chamber of Commerce. 1556 First Street, Napa, CA 94559. 707/226-7455.

Napa Valley Vintners Association. P.O. Box 141, St. Helena, CA 94574. 707/963-0148.

Sonoma County

Sonoma County Convention and Visitors Bureau. 10 Fourth Street, Suite 100, Santa Rosa, CA 95401. 707/575-1191.

Sonoma County Wineries Association. 50 Mark West Spring Road, Suite 303, Santa Rosa, CA 95403. 707/527-7701.

Redwood Empire Association. 785 Market Street, 15th Floor, San Francisco, CA 94103. 415/543-8334.

The Wine Institute. 425 Market Street, Suite 1000, San Francisco, CA 94105. 415/512-0151.

☢ WHERE AND WHEN

Historic Sites

Jack London State Historic Park. 2400 London Ranch Road, Glen Ellen. The park is open 8 AM to sunset daily; the museum 10 AM to 5 PM daily. 707/938-5216.

Lachryma Montis. Spain Street West, Sonoma. Open 10 AM to 5 PM daily. 707/938-1578.

Mission San Francisco Solano. 114 Spain Street East, Sonoma. Open 10 AM to 5 PM daily. 707/938-1519.

Old Faithful Geyser. 1299 Tubbs Lane, Calistoga. Open 9 AM to 6 PM daily in summer, 9 AM to 5 PM daily in winter. 707/942-6463.

Petrified Forest. 4100 Petrified Forest Road, Calistoga. Open 10 AM to 6 PM daily in summer, 10 AM to 5 PM daily in winter. 707/942-6667.

Wineries

Unless noted, the wineries listed offer tastings and tours without an appointment.

Mendocino County wineries include:

Edmeades Vineyards. 3.5 miles north of Philo on Highway 128. Open 10 AM to 6 PM daily June to September, 11 AM to 5 PM daily October to May. 707/895-3232.

Fetzer Vineyards. 1150 Bel Arbes Road, Redwood Valley. By appointment only. The tasting room is on Highway 101 in Hopland. Open 9 AM to 5 PM daily. 707/485-7634.

Handley Cellars. Highway 128, 5 miles north of Philo. By appointment only. 707/895-3876.

Husch Vineyards. Highway 128, 5 miles north of Philo. Open 10 AM to 6 PM daily. 707/895-3216.

Lazy Creek Winery. 4610 Highway 128, 5 miles north of Philo. By appointment only. 707/895-3623.

McDowell Valley Vineyards. 3811 Highway 175, Hopland. Open 10 AM to 6 PM Tuesday to Sunday June 24 through October 1. By appointment only the rest of the year. 707/744-1053.

Navarro Vineyards. Highway 128, 3.5 miles north of Philo. Open 10 AM to 5 PM daily. 707/895-3686.

Pepperwood Springs Winery. Highway 128, 5.5 miles north of Philo. By appointment only. 707/895-2250.

Napa Valley wineries include:

Beringer Vineyards. 2000 Main Street, St. Helena. Open daily 9:30 AM to 5:30 PM (last tour at 4 PM). 707/963-4812.

Charles Krug Winery. 2800 North Main Street, St. Helena. Open 10 AM to 5 PM daily. 707/963-5057.

Christian Brothers/Greystone Cellars. 2555 Main Street, St. Helena. Open 10 AM to 4:30 PM daily. 707/967-3112.

Clos du Val Wine Co. 5330 Silverado Trail, Napa. Open 10 AM to 4 PM daily. 707/252-6711.

Domaine Chandon. California Drive, Yountville. Open 11 AM to 5 PM Wednesday to Sunday. 707/944-2280.

Hans Kornell Champagne Cellars. 1091 Larkmead Lane, St. Helena. Open 10 AM to 4:30 PM daily. 707/963-1237.

Inglenook-Napa Winery. 1991 St. Helena Highway, Rutherford. Open 10 AM to 5 PM daily. 707/967-3362.

Robert Mondavi Winery. 7801 St. Helena Highway, Oakville. Open 9 AM to 5 PM daily. 707/963-9611.

Schramsberg Winery. 1400 Schramsberg Road, Calistoga. Open Monday to Saturday by appointment. 707/942-4558.

Silverado Vineyards. 6121 Silverado Trail, Napa. Open 11 AM to 4 PM daily. 707/257-1770.

Stag's Leap Wine Cellars. 5766 Silverado Trail, Napa. Open 10 AM to 4 PM daily. 707/944-2020.

Sterling Vineyards. 1111 Dunaweal Lane, Calistoga. Open 10:30 AM to 4:30 PM daily. 707/942-5151.

Sonoma County wineries include:

Chalk Hill Winery. 10300 Chalk Hill Road, Healdsburg. By appointment only. 707/838-4306.

Chateau St. Jean. Highway 12 north of Kenwood. Open 10 AM to 4:30 PM daily. 707/833-4134.

Clos du Bois. 5 Fitch Street, Healdsburg. Open 10 AM to 5 PM daily. 707/433-5576.

Estate William Baccala. 4611 Thomas Road, Healdsburg. Open 9 AM to 5 PM daily. 707/433-9463.

F. Korbel and Bros. 13250 River Road, Guerneville. Open 9 AM to 5 PM daily May through September, 8:30 AM to 4:30 PM daily October to April. 707/887-2294.

Glen Ellen Winery. 1883 London Ranch Road, Glen Ellen. Open 10 AM to 4 PM daily. 707/996-1066.

Gloria Ferrer Champagne Caves. 23555 Highway 121, Sonoma. Open 10:30 AM to 4:30 PM daily. 707/996-7256.

Johnson's Alexander Valley Winery. 9333 Highway 128, Healdsburg. Open 10 AM to 5 PM daily. 707/433-2319.

Piper Sonoma Cellars. 11447 Old Redwood Highway, Healdsburg. Open 10 AM to 5 PM daily April through December, 10 AM to 5 PM Friday to Sunday January through March. 707/433-8843.

Sausal Winery. 7370 Highway 128, Healdsburg. Open 10 AM to 4 PM daily. 707/433-2285.

Sebastiani Vineyards. 389 Fourth Street East, Sonoma. Open 10 AM to 5 PM daily. 707/938-5532.

Valley of the Moon Winery. 777 Madrone Road, Glen Ellen. Open 10 AM to 5 PM daily except Thursday, when it's closed. 707/996-6941.

❂ ROMANTIC RETREATS

There are a number of great inns and restaurants in this area. Here are our favorites, but first an explanation of our breakdown of cost categories.

One night in a hotel, resort, or inn for two:

Inexpensive	Less than $75
Moderate	$75 to $125
Expensive	More than $125

Dinner for two (drinks not included):

Inexpensive	less than $25
Moderate	$25 to $60
Expensive	More than $60

Mendocino County: Romantic Lodging

✪ *Albion River Inn.* The location—a cliff overlooking the sea—is stunning and matched by the antique-filled decor in this lovely inn's 20 rooms. Moderate/expensive. Six miles south of Mendocino on Highway 1. Albion, CA 95410. 707/937-1919.

✪ *Glendeven.* The 12 rooms (8 in the main house, 4 in the annex) are charming, filled with a mixture of country furniture and whimsical art. Moderate. 8221 North Highway 1, Little River, CA 95456. 707/937-0083.

✪ *Headlands Inn.* It was a barbershop, a saloon, a hotel annex, and a private home. And then it was moved to its present site. This three-story Victorian inn offers five guest rooms (four in the house, one in an adjacent cottage), all with fireplaces and antique furnishings and either a garden or ocean view. Breakfast is exceptional. Moderate. P.O. Box 132, Mendocino, CA 95460. 707/937-4431.

✪ *Howard Creek Ranch.* There are three rooms (two share a bath) in this New England–style house on a small ranch in a secluded valley east of Mendocino and two additional rooms in a converted boat and a rustic cabin. The rooms are furnished with country pieces. Ask for a room in the main house. Moderate. Highway 1, three miles north of Westport. P.O. Box 121, Westport, CA 95488. 707/964-6725.

✪ *Joshua Grindle Inn.* This inn would be at home on the coast of Maine. It's surrounded by a white picket fence, the furniture is Early American, and the quilts were handmade in New England. There are five guest rooms in the house—three in a new water-tower-like structure and two in a cottage in the back. Moderate. 44800 Little Lake Road, P.O. Box 647, Mendocino, CA 95460. 707/937-4143.

✪ *MacCallum House.* Considered the finest Victorian house in the town, this inn offers 12 rooms in the main house and 9 in cottages around a garden. All the rooms are decorated with Victorian period furnishings. Moderate/expensive. 45020 Albion Street, Box 206, Mendocino, CA 95460. 707/937-0289.

✪ *Mendocino Farmhouse.* White picket fence; gardens of sweet william, candytufts, and other delicate flowers; a two-story farmhouse; fairly new but as comfortable as grandma's house make this three-room inn a special find. Inexpensive. On Olson Lane, off the Comptche-Ukiah Road east of town. P.O. Box 247, Mendocino, CA 95460. 707/937-0241.

✪ *Mendocino Village Inn.* The 12 guest rooms in this Queen Anne Victorian inn are furnished in an eclectic mix. Ten of the rooms have private baths (two share a bath), seven have fireplaces, and several have private entrances. Each room has a different decor, ranging from Indian (the Quilt Room) to Victorian (the Diamond Lil Room) to nautical (Captain's Quarters). Moderate. 44860 Main Street, Box 626, Mendocino, CA 95460. 707/937-0246.

✪ *1021 Main Street.* Unusual, to say the least. This four-room inn (two in the main house, two in the cottages called the Foundry and the Zen House) offers privacy, fantastic views of the ocean, and unusual objets d'art. Moderate. 1021 Main Street, Mendocino, CA 95460. 707/937-5150.

✪ *Stanford Inn by the Sea.* Facing the Pacific and overlooking the town of Mendocino, this rustic inn has the feel of a mountain lodge despite an abundance of luxury. The 25 rooms have wood walls and ceilings, wood-burning stoves and fireplaces, country furnishings including four-poster beds, and floral prints. Each room has a balcony or patio. A Cape Cod–style cottage offers two bedrooms, a full kitchen, and a living room. Moderate/expensive. Southeast of town on the Comptche-Ukiah Road, P.O. Box 487, Mendocino, CA 95460. 707/937-5615.

✪ *Toll House Inn.* One of the few inns in the heart of Mendocino's wine country, the Toll House is a 1912 Victorian inn with five spacious rooms. All the rooms have fireplaces, and three have private baths. The inn has gardens and a hot tub. Expensive. P.O. Box 268, Boonville, CA 94515. 707/895-3630.

✪ *Whitegate Inn.* The five guest rooms in this elegant inn have fireplaces and are furnished with antiques and decorated with lace curtains and other tasteful fabrics. The gazebo is popular for weddings. Moderate. 499 Howard Street, P.O. Box 150, Mendocino, CA 95460. 707/937-4892.

Mendocino County: Fine Dining

✪ *Albion River Inn.* Continental fare featuring seafood and pasta at this lovely bed-and-breakfast. Expensive. 3790 North Highway 1, Albion. 707/937-1919.

✪ *Cafe Beaujolais.* Superb (and calorie-laden) country cooking at this rustic spot. Breakfast and lunch daily, dinner Thursday through Sunday. Moderate. 961 Ukiah Street. 707/937-5614.

✪ *MacCallum House.* Fine continental dining in a very charming Victorian bed-and-breakfast. Moderate. 45020 Albion Street. 707/937-5763.

✪ *955 Ukiah Street Restaurant.* Californian cuisine—fresh vegetables, pastas, and the like—served up with flair. Moderate. 955 Ukiah Street. Moderate. 707/937-1955.

✪ *Sea Gull.* Popular with locals, this casual restaurant serves up excellent omelets as well as fish and meat dishes. Moderate. Lansing and Ukiah streets. Moderate. 707/937-2100.

Napa Valley: Romantic Lodging

✪ *Auberge du Soleil.* Perhaps the finest inn in the Napa Valley, this 38-room retreat is certainly the most romantic. The 29 rooms and 19 suites are spacious and tastefully decorated. The resort has a pool and tennis courts. Expensive. 180 Rutherford Hill Road, Rutherford, CA 94573. 707/963-1211.

✪ *Beazley House.* This shingled Colonial Revival house was built in 1902, and its elegant stained-glass windows, hardwood floors, and wainscoting remain well-preserved today. The nine rooms, all with private baths, are cozy and comfortably furnished. Moderate. 1910 First Street, Napa, CA 94559. 707/257-1649.

✪ *Coombes Residence.* This brown shingled house is one of Napa's oldest homes. It was built around 1852, and now offers four rooms, all nicely furnished with wrought iron beds and Oriental rugs. The rooms share 2½ baths. There is a pool and jacuzzi. Moderate. 720 Seminary, Napa, CA 94559. 707/257-0789.

✪ *Culver's, A Country Inn.* This 1870s Victorian inn has seven guest rooms nicely furnished with antiques of the period. The rooms share three baths. Moderate. 1805 Foothill Boulevard, Calistoga, CA 94515. 707/942-4535.

✪ *The Foothill House.* There are three beautiful rooms in this remodeled turn-of-the-century home. Each room is furnished with country antiques and has a private bath and private entrance. The best is the Evergreen Suite, with a deck, jacuzzi, and a view of Mt. St. Helena. Moderate/expensive. 3037 Foothill Boulevard, Calistoga, CA 94515. 707/942-6933.

✪ *Gallery Osgood.* Beautiful Victorian furnishings make the three guest rooms in this century-old Queen Anne–style home a pleasant place to rest from the rigors of tastings. Moderate. 2230 First Street, Napa, CA 94559. 707/224-0100.

✪ *Hennessey House.* There are five wonderful rooms in this 1889 Queen Anne Victorian inn and four more in its carriage house. All of the rooms have private baths, four have whirlpool baths, and two have fireplaces. The rooms are furnished with beautiful antiques. Expensive. 1727 Main Street, Napa, CA 94559. 707/226-3774.

✪ *Hope-Bosworth* and *Hope-Merrill.* These two homes across from each other are very different architecturally. The Hope-Bosworth House was built around 1880 and is a Victorian with Eastlake touches. The Hope-Merrill House is a patternbook house built in 1904. The former has five beautifully furnished rooms, the latter seven. Moderate. 21238 Geyserville Avenue, Geyserville, CA 95441. 707/857-3356.

✪ *Larkmead Country Inn.* Located next to the Hans Kornell Champagne Cellars, this delightful inn has four rooms, all comfortably furnished and with private baths. Moderate. 1103 Lark-mead Lane, Calistoga, CA 94515. 707/942-5360.

✪ *Magnolia Hotel.* This brick and stone 12-room hotel was built in 1873 and has served as a bordello and a speakeasy in years past. Today it is a romantic and elegant retreat, with the rooms offering brass or iron beds, handmade quilts, private baths, and wonderful views. There is a heated pool and jacuzzi out back. Expensive. 6529 Yount Street, Yountville, CA 94599. 707/944-2056.

✪ *Meadowood Resort Hotel.* Surrounded by vineyards, this mag-nificent 250-acre resort offers 24 rooms and 48 suites, all very elegantly furnished. Facilities include a pool, tennis, and 9-hole golf course. Expensive. 900 Meadwood Lane, St. Helena, CA 94574. 707/963-3646 and 800/458-8080 nationwide.

✪ *Napa Valley Railway Inn.* Nine vintage railway cars make up this unusual inn. The cars have been converted into luxurious suites. All have private baths, skylights, and brass beds. Moderate. 6503 Washington Street, Yountville, CA 94599. 707/944-2000.

✪ *Old World Inn.* The innkeepers are British, and it shows at tea time when Scottish shortbread and date pinwheels are served. This feast is followed by a wine-tasting hour, with the appropriate vintages and cheeses. There are eight nicely furnished rooms, each with a private bath. Expensive. 1301 Jefferson Street, Napa, CA 94559. 707/257-0112.

✪ *Oliver House.* This three-story chalet offers four rooms filled with antiques from England and Scotland. The rooms have private baths, and three have views of the vineyards in the nearby hills. Expensive. 2970 Silverado Trail North, St. Helena, CA 94574. 707/963-4089.

✪ *La Residence Country Inn.* Everything about this 1870 blue-with-white-trim Gothic Revival is elegant. The nine guest rooms, seven with private baths, are stuffed with antiques. Most of the rooms have fireplaces and all have sitting areas. The two acres of grounds are well shaded by fruit trees, and a heated pool and jacuzzi await to soothe the tired traveler. Expensive. 4066 St. Helena Highway North, Napa, CA 94558. 707/253-0337.

✪ *Silverado Country Club.* This luxury 1,200-acre resort offers 270 condominium units—from one to three bedrooms. Facilities include 7 pools, 20 tennis courts, and 2 Robert Trent Jones golf courses. Expensive. 1600 Atlas Peak Road, Napa, CA 94558. 707/257-0200 and 800/532-0500 nationwide.

✪ *Villa St. Helena.* This huge terracotta-roof villa has three suites, all very elegantly furnished. Each has a private bath. The villa also has a pool and a courtyard filled with flowers. Expensive. 2727 Sulphur Springs Avenue, St. Helena, CA 94574. 707/ 963-2514.

✪ *The White Ranch.* This charming farmhouse was built around the end of the Civil War. It offers a pleasant room, with a private bath and dressing area. Moderate. 707 White Lane, St. Helena, CA 94574. 707/963-4635.

✪ *Wine Country Inn.* This hilltop inn has 25 rooms with private balconies, hand-painted canopy beds (or Victorian beds modified to accept a queen-size mattress), and private baths. Fifteen of the rooms have fireplaces. Expensive. 1152 Lodi Lane, St. Helena, CA 94574. 707/963-7077.

Napa Valley: Fine Dining

✪ *Auberge du Soleil.* The service can be spotty, but the French country fare at this elegant resort is outstanding! Expensive. 180 Rutherford Hill Road, Rutherford. 707/963-1211.

✪ *California Cafe.* Creative Californian cuisine in a casual dining room. You may eat on the terrace when the weather is nice. Moderate. 6795 Washington Street, Yountville. 707/944-2330.

✪ *Calistoga Inn.* Excellent seafood and Californian cuisine. Expensive. 1250 Lincoln Avenue, Calistoga. 707/942-4101.

✪ *The Diner.* Sensational Mexican dishes at inexpensive prices. 6476 Washington Street, Yountville. 707/944-2626.

✪ *Domaine Chandon.* The winery is also one of the area's finest restaurants, serving classic Italian dishes with a Californian touch. Expensive. California Drive, off the Yountville Cross Road, Yountville. 707/944-2892.

✪ *French Laundry.* Don't be misled by the name. This beautiful dining room serves a prix-fixe five-course dinner featuring creative French cuisine. Expensive. 6640 Washington Street, Yountville. 707/944-2380.

✪ *Mustards Grill.* Creative Californian cuisine served in a festive atmosphere. Moderate. 7399 St. Helena Highway, Yountville. 707/944-2424.

✪ *Oakville Grocery Co.* If you are planning to picnic during your tour of the wineries, this fantastic gourmet food store is the place to stop first. Great breads, fine cheese, and excellent smoked fish and meats make a memorable meal. The cost depends on your appetite. 7856 St. Helena Highway, Oakville. 707/944-8802.

✪ *Piatti.* Light Italian fare and great pizza. Moderate. 6480 Washington Street, Yountville. 707/944-2070.

✪ *Silverado Country Club.* Wonderful American fare—steaks, seafood, and the like—served in a formal dining room. Expensive. 1600 Atlas Peak Road, Napa. 707/257-0200.

✪ *Terra.* The setting is a century-old stone foundry, the ambiance is casual and the cuisine is American with a hint of Japan and Italy. Moderate. 1345 Railroad Avenue, St. Helena. 707/ 963-8931.

✪ *Tra Vigne.* Great pizzas and pastas in a barn converted into a trattoria. Moderate. 1050 Charter Oak Avenue, St. Helena. 707/963-4444.

Sonoma County: Romantic Lodging

✪ *Camellia.* This Italianate Victorian inn, built in 1869, has nine rooms, seven with private baths. Each room is furnished with antiques of mid-1800s. Moderate. 211 North Street, Healdsburg, CA 95448. 707/433-8182.

✪ *Chalet Bed and Breakfast.* This two-story Swiss-style chalet offers four rooms, two up and two down, that share two baths. The rooms are furnished with a mix of antiques and collectibles. Moderate. 18935 Fifth Street West, Sonoma, CA 95476. 707/ 996-0190.

✪ *Haydon House.* There are six rooms in the main inn, but the real delight at this lovely retreat are the two rooms in the blue-and-white Victorian cottage hidden away in the gardens and trees in back. You will find huge jacuzzis, antiques out of a Victorian fantasy, and lovely flowers everywhere. The eight rooms share four baths. Moderate. 321 Haydon Street, Healdsburg, CA 95448. 707/433-5228.

✪ *Madrona Manor.* One of the most elegant inns in Sonoma, this mansion, built in 1881 as a vacation home, is now a fantastic retreat in the wine country. The rooms are large and elegantly furnished with fine antiques. There are 20 rooms, all with private baths and 9 with fireplaces. Nine of the rooms are in the manor and the rest are in the carriage house and adjacent buildings. The best rooms are in the mansion. Expensive. 1001 Westside Road, Box 919, Healdsburg, CA 95448. 707/433-4231.

✪ *Ye Olde Shelford House.* After breakfast, you can get into a horse-drawn carriage for a tour and tasting at the wineries in the lovely countryside near this restored 1885 Victorian house. The inn offers three rooms, two with private baths. The rooms are furnished with family antiques and heirlooms. Moderate. 29955 River Road, Cloverdale, CA 95425. 707/894-5956.

✪ *Overview Farm.* The three guest rooms in this 1880s farmhouse are spacious and well furnished with early American antiques and collectibles. Each room has a private bath. Moderate. 15650 Arnold Drive, Sonoma, CA 94576. 707/938-8574.

✪ *Pygmalion House.* This cozy Victorian house in the center of Santa Rosa's historic district offers five nice rooms. The rooms are furnished with French Provincial pieces, plush carpeting, and old-fashioned bathroom fixtures in the private baths. Inexpensive. 331 Orange Street, Santa Rosa, CA 95401. 707/526-3407.

✪ *Ridenhour Ranch House Inn.* This redwood ranch house is a short walk from the Korbel Winery. The house offers eight rooms, five with private baths. The rooms are stylishly furnished with American and European antiques. Moderate. 12850 River Road, Guerneville, CA 95446. 707/887-1033.

✪ *Sonoma Mission Inn.* This elegant inn is a merger of early Californian architecture and classic Mediterranean style. There are 170 luxurious rooms and an elegant and complete spa. Expensive. 18140 Sonoma Highway, Sonoma, CA 95476. 707/938-9000; and 800/862-4945 in California, 800/358-9022 elsewhere in the United States.

❂ *Timberhill Ranch.* One of the most beautiful and luxurious resorts on the northern coast, this elegant country inn offers 10 secluded cottages, all very spacious and romantic. The rooms have fireplaces and antique furnishings. Facilities include a pool and jacuzzi surrounded by a forest, tennis courts, and a fantastic restaurant. Room rates include breakfast and six-course dinner. Expensive, and well worth it. 35755 Hauser Bridge Road, Cazadero, CA 95421. 707/847-3258.

Sonoma County: Fine Dining

❂ *Les Arcades.* This small and pretty restaurant serves superb French dishes and even better desserts. Expensive. 133 East Napa Street, Sonoma. 707/938-3723.

❂ *La Casa.* The specialties of the house are the wisest choices at this excellent Mexican restaurant. Inexpensive. 121 East Spain Street, Sonoma. 707/996/3406.

❂ *Chateau Souverain Restaurant at the Winery.* Excellent continental and Californian cuisine served in a room with a view of the vineyards. Expensive. 400 Souverain Road, Geyserville. 707/433-3141.

❂ *Depot Hotel 1870.* This hotel's beautifully restored dining room serves up superb northern Italian cuisine as well as very creative Californian dishes. The chef-owner has won a number of awards. Moderate. 241 First Street West, Sonoma. 707/938-2980.

❂ *Madrona Manor.* This beautiful inn also has a wonderful dining room, serving creative Californian cuisine. Expensive. 1001 Westside Road, Healdsburg. 707/433-4231.

✪ *Ma Stokeld's Village Pub.* This is an English pub, complete with bangers, English pasties (turnovers with meat and other fillings), pork pies, and other delicacies. Inexpensive. 464 First Street East, Sonoma. 707/935-0660.

✪ *Sonoma Hotel.* Exceptional beef, seafood, and pasta at this charming restoration of an 1880s dining room. Moderate. 110 West Spain Street, Sonoma. 707/996-2996.

✪ *Sonoma Mission Inn.* Nouvelle Californian cuisine, with an emphasis on seafood and poultry. Expensive. 18140 Highway 12, Boyes Hot Springs. 707/938-9000.

Chapter Three

Coastal Cruising

Every so often, we discover a place that is so dramatically beautiful that everything associated with it is fixed forever in our memories. Even today, we can relive even the tiniest details—what we had for breakfast, the scent of the wildflowers, the view from the inns, the color of the sea—of our drives along California's coast.

The coastline from Oregon to Morro Rock is everything that is beautiful and romantic. It's a shore where you will find forests of towering redwoods—John Steinbeck called them "ambassadors from another time"—as well as groves of pygmy trees. Here you will discover the rugged beauty of sea-battered rocky black cliffs and coves as well as small seaports and villages that celebrate their heritage and proudly display their architectural beauty. You can also see gentle, grass-covered hills shrouded by fog and a castle that is a testament to one man's mania.

Two roads take you to these sights. From Marin County to Oregon, first Highway 1 and then Highway 101 are the paths to glory. From the Monterey Peninsula to Morro Rock, Highway 1 is the drive of choice.

Whether you take both drives or just one, you will be changed forever. The scenery is magnificent, the towns are colorful and enticing, and the sights will last forever in your memories and in your hearts.

✪ FROM THE GOLDEN GATE TO OREGON

When you cross the Golden Gate Bridge, you leave behind the busy, sophisticated world of San Francisco and enter a region no less beautiful, but far more peaceful. The 400 miles of coast from the Golden Gate to Oregon are magnificent: windswept shores, small fishing and lumbering communities, majestic forests over-shadowed by the towering redwoods, and wild rivers.

The first stop on a tour of the North Coast is Sausalito, a colorful waterfront community where art galleries, houseboats, century-old Victorian mansions, and modern villas share the best view of San Francisco.

Take Highway 1/101 to the Sausalito exit, then drive south on Bridgeway, the main boulevard of this community. The center of Sausalito is the waterfront near Bridgeway and Spinnaker Drive, where the ferry from San Francisco docks near the Sausalito Hotel, a renovated mission-style building filled with lovely Victo-rian antiques. From this point, you can wander along Bridgeway and explore the many wonderful shops and galleries. A good place to start is The Village Fair (777 Bridgeway), a maze with more than two dozen shops and restaurants.

However, not all the sights are in the shops. On the streets higher on the hill you can see some of the Victorian homes built around the turn of the century. They are privately owned, but you can sightsee from the street. The houseboats that add color to Sausalito's waterfront can be seen on Richardson Bay, north of

✪ The Lone Cypress, a famous landmark on the Monterey Peninsula. (Courtesy of Monterey Visitors and Convention Bureau)

Marinship Park on Bridgeway. You can continue driving north on Bridgeway to Highway 1/101 and the nearby community of Tiburon. Less well known than Sausalito, Tiburon is a small town with fashionable shops, cafes, and galleries along its Main Street.

Return to Highway 1/101 and continue north to the Highway 1

exit. Take it and follow Highway 1 north to the turnoff for Muir Woods National Monument, a 550-acre park that is home to stands of awe-inspiring redwood trees. The Cathedral and Bohemian groves at the entrance to the park have redwoods that are more than 1,000 years old, 250 feet high, and 12 feet wide. More redwoods can be found at Mt. Tamalpais State Park, next to Muir Woods. Next to the two parks are the most popular beaches in Marin County—Muir and Stinson beaches. Muir Beach can be reached by taking the Vista Point turnoff while Stinson Beach, larger and nicer than Muir, can be reached by taking the road over Mt. Tamalpais.

Besides the two parks and beaches, other nature preserves are nearby. The Audubon Canyon Ranch, a 1,000-acre bird sanctuary, is 3 miles north of Stinson on Highway 1. The 73,000-acre Point Reyes National Seashore, which offers miles of dunes and wind-swept beaches, is one of the loveliest sections of the Pacific coast. The park's Bear Valley Visitors Center on Highway 1 near Olema offers more information and exhibits and it is the center of the area's hiking trails. The Miwok Indian Village, which is a reconstruction, is a short walk from the center.

Continue driving north to Jenner. The coast up until now has been dramatically beautiful, but it was just setting the stage for the 20 miles north of Jenner. Here the coast becomes more rugged, with Highway 1 forced to make hairpin turns. There are frequent turnoffs allowing visitors to admire the views of the Pacific and the rocky shore. The scenery is fantastic, so take the time to stop and enjoy it.

Fort Ross, the first sign of civilization north of Jenner, is a reconstructed fortress built by Russian seal hunters in 1812. The park displays a chapel, barracks, stockade, and museum.

Farther north is Salt Pond State Park, a picturesque stop where you can often see seals; the Kruse Rhododendron Reserve just north of Fisk Mill Cove; and Gualala Point Regional Park, a popular place for whale watching and camping.

In Point Arena is the Point Arena Lighthouse, a 115-foot structure that offers stunning views of the coast and sea. At Little River, watch for the turn to Van Damme State Park. The park is 3 miles inland. The Pygmy Forest is in the southeast corner of this park. Because of the soil, roots are prevented from going deep into the earth, and this results in stunted trees. The pygmy trees, some more than two centuries old, may have trunks that are only one-quarter inch in diameter and a height measured in a few feet.

The next major town on this coast is Mendocino, a lovely community with architecture similar to that of a turn-of-the-century Maine seaport. Mendocino is the center of tourism on the northern coast and is famous for its cozy inns, elegant Victorian homes, and creative restaurants. (For more details, see Chapter One.)

Ten miles north of Mendocino is Fort Bragg, a haven for commercial fishing boats and the boats that make trips to see the gray whales that migrate past every December. Fort Bragg's fishing heritage is celebrated every July when the community holds "The World's Largest Salmon Barbecue." It's great fun, and even better food.

Fort Bragg is also home to the California Western Railroad, a former logging line that now offers excursion tours into Willits 40 miles inland. The line has the nickname "The Skunk Railroad" because in its early years it ran on gas and left an awful smell in its wake.

North of Fort Bragg, Highway 1 turns inland into timber country before joining Highway 101 at Leggett—the gateway to the Redwood Empire.

The first redwood forest you will encounter is the Drive-Thru Tree Park, just off Highway 101 in Leggett. This is the famous redwood tree that has a road tunnel through its trunk. North of town is the Richardson Grove State Park, another impressive forest of redwoods. The best way to experience these mammoth trees is to take the Avenue of the Giants, Route 254 off Highway 101 north of Garberville. This scenic 33-mile drive takes you past some of the tallest trees on earth. The road cuts through part of the Humboldt Redwoods State Park, another preserve offering more than 50,000 acres of wilderness and rivers. The tallest tree in Humboldt Park is slightly over 360 feet and is located in the Founders Grove.

These massive forests led to uncontrolled logging and massive fortunes in decades past. Now, the logging is controlled somewhat, and the former timber barons have left behind some magnificent mansions. Continue north on Highway 101 to the turnoff for Ferndale. Some of the most beautiful Victorian homes in the state can be found in this former logging boomtown. A bit farther north is Eureka, another logging town that has about 100 elegant Victorian mansions dating from its nineteenth-century boom days. Eureka is also home to numerous artists, who display their creations at the Old Town Art Guild Cooperative (233 F Street).

These two towns, Ferndale and Eureka, are worth at least a stop for lunch and shopping, if not an overnight stay for a longer look at their many fine homes and art galleries. A must stop is the Carson Mansion, at Second and M streets in Eureka's Old Town. Carson was a lumber baron and his majestic Victorian mansion was built in 1884–86 and is called the most photographed house in America.

Whenever you leave these gems, continue driving north to Redwood National Park, which is made up of three state preserves: Del Norte Coast Redwoods, Jedediah Smith Redwoods, and Praire Creek Redwoods. The park is more than 40 miles long and covers 106,000 acres.

The visitors center for the park is in Orick. There you can pick up more information about trails, wildlife sanctuaries, and special events in the park.

North of the Redwood Empire is Crescent City, a fishing port famed for its crab and salmon. A short drive farther north is Oregon, and all its wonders.

Before you leave this lovely part of the world, take time to go to the parking area near the entrance to the Praire Creek Park. From this lookout, visitors can often get glimpses of a herd of majestic elk that live in this wilderness. As you look down on the elk, the busy, sophisticated streets of San Francisco seem far, far away.

✪ FROM MONTEREY BAY TO MORRO ROCK

The Monterey Peninsula is the gateway to some of the most dramatic and unforgettable landscape in the nation. On this central coast of California you will see missions that date back to the beginning of Spanish colonization, small towns filled with art galleries and fine inns, quaint communities celebrated by writers such as Robert Louis Stevenson and John Steinbeck, and, if that isn't enough, a castle that seems like it belongs in a fairytale.

From 1770 to 1822, Monterey was the capital of Spanish California. When Mexico revolted and won its independence, Monterey remained the capital of Mexican California until 1846, when Commodore John Sloat arrived in Monterey and claimed California for the United States.

Monterey's historic heritage can be seen in Monterey State Historic Park (20 Custom House Plaza). These nineteenth-century buildings date back to California's early years and include a Customs House (1 Custom House Plaza); Pacific House, a former saloon (10 Custom House Plaza); the Joseph Boston Store, founded in 1849 (Scott and Olivers streets); the Larkin House, which blends New England and Mexico styles into a synthesis called Monterey style (Jefferson Street and Calle Principal); Cooper-Molera Adobe, a large complex that offers gardens, a gift shop, and an adobe home dating back to 1820 (Polk and Munras streets); and the Stevenson House, where the author lived briefly (530 Houston Street).

The Casa Soberanes (336 Pacific Street) once housed the Spanish military commander and Colton Hall (Pacific between Madison and Jefferson streets) is where the state's constitution was drafted.

Not every attraction in Monterey is historic. The Monterey Peninsula Museum of Art across from Colton Hall displays works by Ansel Adams and other local photographers and artists.

Steinbeck made Monterey and its waterfront famous in his novel *Cannery Row*. The waterfront has seen better (and worse) times. Fisherman's Wharf (885 Abrego Street) is crowded with tourists, but there is no better place to see or feed the cute and playful sea lions and otters that make this shore their home. This is also the place to arrange for a fascinating whale-watching trip during the winter months.

Cannery Row, whose center is in the 400 block of Cannery Row street, was a booming sardine processing district when Steinbeck wrote about it in 1944. Since then, the sardines disappeared, forcing the processing plants to close. The area slowly turned shabby but has enjoyed a renaissance in recent years when the canneries were refurbished and converted into attractive waterfront shopping and dining arcades. A pleasant way to break away from shopping is a stop at the tasting rooms of two wineries—Bargetto and Paul Masson—in Cannery Row.

The driving force behind this waterfront renaissance is the new Monterey Bay Aquarium (886 Cannery Row). The aquarium has a number of fascinating exhibits and is usually very crowded on weekends.

Other sights on this lovely peninsula include the town of Pacific Grove, established in 1875 as a summer retreat for various religious denominations. Pacific Grove is home not only to some beautiful and well-preserved Victorian homes, but also to millions of black-and-orange monarch butterflies that spend October through March in the town's pine groves. These annual visitors have given Pacific Grove the title of "Butterfly Town U.S.A." The butterflies are spectacular and can be viewed, often hanging in clumps from tree limbs, from Washington Park at Alder Street and Pine Avenue.

Pacific Grove has 3 miles of spectacular coastline, and the best way to enjoy it is by walking, biking, or driving along Ocean View Boulevard. The boulevard is lined with many fine Victorian homes that have wonderful views of the Pacific.

Finally, before leaving the Monterey Peninsula, head to Lighthouse Avenue and the entrance to 17-Mile Drive, the most stunning coastal road in the nation. There is a $5 entrance fee, but it's well worth it, for you will see the lone cypress, the solitary, twisted tree on a rocky finger of land made famous by photographers; world-class golf courses like Spyglass Hill and Pebble Beach; million-dollar mansions and two islands—Seal Rock and Bird Rock—that are home to sea lions, seals, cormorants, and pelicans. This drive ends in Carmel, a quaint and colorful community that is filled with art galleries, fine shops, numerous inns, and excellent restaurants. (See Chapter One for more details.)

After Carmel, Highway 1 heads south into Big Sur Country, a dramatically beautiful region that moved Henry Miller to write: "If the soul were to choose an arena in which to stage its agonies, this would be the place for it. One feels exposed—not only to the elements, but to the sight of God."

You can get a look at what Miller was talking about at the Bixby Creek Bridge, 13 miles south of Carmel. Stop at the parking area on the north side of the bridge and walk to the edge for stunning views of the coast and picture taking.

Five miles beyond the bridge is the Point Sur Light Station, a clifftop beacon. Tours are offered Sundays at 9:30 AM. A bit farther south is Julia Pfeiffer Burns State Park, where you can take short hikes to see redwoods, a waterfall, or the beach. The shore is lovely, but the waters are too rough and cold for swimming.

By now, development has been left behind and the majesty of the Big Sur becomes visible: the towering St. Lucia Mountains, often shrouded in fog, meeting a rugged, rocky shore battered by ceaseless waves.

From the Julia Pfeiffer Burns Park, the Big Sur stretches on for miles, with each new cove and slope offering ever more captivating views. The scenery is magnificent, and is an appropriate buildup to a man-made wonder found 90 miles south of Carmel, at the south end of the Big Sur coast. There you will find San Simeon and the Hearst Castle. Publisher William Randolph Hearst built his castle atop "La Cuesta Encantada" (Enchanted Hill). Construction started on the 100-room castle in 1919 and wasn't completed until 1947—four years before Hearst's death.

"Pleasure," Hearst said, "is worth what you can afford to pay for it." In the case of the castle, "pleasure" cost more than three million Depression-era dollars. For Hearst, the castle was more than a home. It was a showcase for his enormous collection of fine art, a place to house and entertain his entourage and visiting friends, and an estate to show the world how powerful and rich he was.

The castle is magnificent, and that is an understatement. The castle—known as Casa Grande but informally called San Simeon—is surrounded by formal Renaissance gardens. It has twin towers, a huge "noble room" with hand-carved sixteenth-

century Spanish and eighteenth-century Italian ceilings, and statues of saints, priceless fifteenth-century Flemish tapestries, artworks, and other sculptures, a lavish theater, three luxurious
guest houses, and pools (a Byzantine indoor pool surrounded by
marble copies of famous statues), fountains, and other fantasylike
attractions. There is even a zoo. Once the 2,000-acre preserve
contained the world's largest private zoo. Now it holds only a few
elk, zebras, deer, and goats.

The castle is now a state park. The visitors center offers films
on Hearst and his castle, and tours of the estate usually require
advance reservations. (Call 619/452-1950 and 800/444-7275 nationwide.)

After this dream estate, the small town of Cambria seems
overshadowed by the luxury and vastness that is the Hearst castle.
Cambria, though, is lovely, but a quick return to earth. Cambria is
filled with Victorian homes and art galleries and studios. Nearby
Leffingwell's Landing is a state park where you can watch otters
and explore tidal pools.

The last stop on this coastal drive is an extinct volcano—
Morro Rock. Created 20 million years ago, this 576-foot-high rock
stands guard over Morro Bay. You can drive across the 4.5-mile-
long finger of sand and rock that connects the mainland to the
rock. The rock is now a sanctuary for the peregrine falcons that
nest there.

The town of Morro Bay is small, but has some fine shops and
restaurants at the Embarcadero (895 Napa Street). The Centennial
Staircase (535 Harbor Street) is made of redwood taken from two
water tanks that served the city for 50 years, and a giant concrete
chessboard, with pieces also made of redwood. You can play a
game with the oversize pieces for a small fee.

A short drive away from the rock is the town of San Luis
Obispo. This town has some historic sights—the Mission (782

Golf Where the Pros Play

The Monterey Peninsula has been called the golf capital of the world. There are 20 courses on the Peninsula, and several of them are internationally famous.

Located inside 17-Mile Drive, the Pebble Beach Golf Links is the site of each year's AT&T Pro-Am, where the PGA pros play with Hollywood and sports celebrities. Two nearby courses are just as famous. Spyglass Hill and Spanish Bay Golf Links are known for challenging holes and un-challenged views of the ocean. The greens fees at these courses start at about $100 a person. Call 408/624-3811 or contact your hotel concierge to get a tee time. (Note: The Japanese conglomerate that recently bought Pebble Beach may turn the course into a private club.)

Other peninsula golf courses that will challenge your skills include the new Poppy Hills (408/625-2035), already rated in the world's top 20 by Golf Digest. As old as Poppy Hill is young is the Old Del Monte Golf Course (408/373-2436), the first course west of the Mississippi.

For spectacular scenery and lower greens fees, you may enjoy playing the Pacific Grove Golf Links (408/375-3456).

Monterey Street) dates from 1772 and the Ah Louis store (800 Palm Street) served the Chinese railroad workers in the 1880s when the town was called San Luis Obispo de Tolosa. But not even these places can match the inn that has made the town famous to travelers around the world. The Madonna Inn (100 Madonna Road) is a castle with winding staircases, turrets, and 109 rooms—each with what one would call "individual decor." The rooms are fantasies, and are decorated in different themes. The Love Nest, for example, is a pink dream (or nightmare), the Cave Man has a leopard-skin bedspread and a waterfall shower, while the Safari Room has a big-game-hunter theme. You get the picture. It's, well, unusual.

Back at Morro Rock, romance needs no fantasy. As the sun

drops, the sandy finger of land leading to this west coast Gibraltar is the perfect place to watch the sky change colors and the stars fill the night.

✪ FOR MORE INFORMATION

North Coast

Eureka Chamber of Commerce. 2112 Broadway, Eureka, CA 95501. 707/442-3738 and 800/356-6381 nationwide.

Fort Bragg Chamber of Commerce. 332 North Main Street, P.O. Box 1141, Fort Bragg, CA 95437. 707/964-3153.

Redwood Empire Association. One Market Plaza, Spear Street Tower No. 1001, San Francisco, CA 04105. 415/543-8334. (This office gives information for the entire north coast.)

Sausalito Chamber of Commerce. 333 Caledonia Street, P.O. Box 566, Sausalito, CA 94966. 415/332-0505.

Central Coast

Big Sur Chamber of Commerce. P.O. Box 87, Big Sur, CA 93920. 408/667-2100.

Monterey Peninsula Visitors and Convention Bureau. 320 Alvarado Street, P.O. Box 1770, Monterey, CA 93942. 408/649-1770.

San Simeon Chamber of Commerce. P.O. Box 1, San Simeon, CA 93542. 805/927-3500.

✪ WHERE AND WHEN

North Coast

Avenue of the Giants. Scenic Route 254 in Humboldt Redwoods State Park. 707/946-2311.

California Western Railroad. Scenic excursions into the redwood forests daily. Fort Bragg. 707/964-6371.

Drive-Thru Tree Park. Leggett. 707/925-6363.

Muir Woods National Monument. 17 miles north of Mill Valley on Highway 1. Open 8 AM to sunset daily. 415/388-2595.

Point Reyes National Seashore. Off Highway 1 in Point Reyes. Open daily. 415/663-1092.

Redwood Information Center. Orick. Open 9 AM to 5 PM daily. 707/488-3641.

Redwood National Park. 1111 Second Street, Crescent City. Open daily. 707/464-6101.

Central Coast

Cannery Row. 425 Cannery Row, Monterey. Open daily.

Fisherman's Wharf. 885 Abrego Street, Monterey. Open daily.

Hearst San Simeon Historical Monument. P.O. Box 8, San Simeon, 93542. 800/444-7275. Open daily except Thanksgiving, Christmas, and New Year's. For tickets call 800/444-PARK.

Julia Pfeiffer Burns State Park. Highway 1, Big Sur, 37 miles south of Carmel. Open daily. 408/667-2315.

Monterey Bay Aquarium. 886 Cannery Row, Monterey. Open 10 AM to 6 PM daily. Admission fee. 408/757-8085.

Monterey Path of History. Guided tours on the hour to the historic sites in Monterey. 408/649-1770.

Monterey Peninsula Museum of Art. 559 Pacific Street. Open 10 AM to 4 PM Tuesday through Saturday, 1 PM to 4 PM Sunday. 408/372-7591.

Monterey State Historic Park. 20 Custom House Plaza. Tours; hours and days vary. 408/649-2836.

Morro Rock. 895 Napa Street, Morro Bay. 805/772-4467.

The Ferry to Sausalito

There are two ferries from San Francisco to Sausalito. The Golden Gate Ferry leaves from the docks at Market Street and the Embarcadero in San Francisco (415/332-6600). The Red and White Fleet departs from Pier 41 at Fisherman's Wharf (415/546-2896). The trip takes about 20 minutes.

Whale Watching

You can sail off to watch the whales with the following cruise agencies:

Fort Bragg
   Anchor Charter Boats (707/964-4550)

Half Moon Bay
   Captain John's (415/728-3377)
   Oceanic Society Expeditions (415/474-3385)

Monterey
   Chris Fishing Trips (408/375-5951)
   Monterey Sport Fishing (408/372-2203)
   Princess Monterey Cruises (408/372-2628)
   Sam's Fishing Fleet (408/372-0577)

Morro Bay
   Virg's Fish'n Inc. (805/772-1223)

Point Reyes
Point Reyes Field Seminars (415/663-1200)

San Francisco
Oceanic Society Expeditions (415/474-3385)

Santa Barbara
Santa Barbara Museum of Natural History (805/682-4334)
Sea Center (805/962-0885)
Sea Landing Sportfishing (805/963-3564)

✿ ROMANTIC RETREATS

Here are our favorites, but first an explanation of our breakdown
of cost categories follows:

One night in a hotel, resort, or inn for two:

Inexpensive	Less than $75
Moderate	$75 to $125
Expensive	More than $125

For dinner for two (drinks not included):

Inexpensive	Less than $25
Moderate	$25 to $60
Expensive	More than $60

North Coast, by City: Romantic Lodging and Fine Dining

Elk: Romantic Lodging

✿ *Elk Cove Inn.* This lovely Victorian inn offers its guests nine
elegant rooms, private paths to the nearby beaches, and lots of
serenity. The rooms are in the main house and two annexes. All

are comfortable, and seven have private baths. Moderate/
expensive. 6300 South Highway 1, Elk, CA 95432. 707/877-3321.

Elk: Fine Dining

✪ *Harbor House.* Very good continental cuisine, but the views of
the sea and the coast are even better. Expensive. 5600 South
Highway 1, 6 miles south of Highway 128. 707/877-3203.

Eureka: Romantic Lodging

✪ *Carter House* and *Hotel Carter.* These two recent creations by
innkeeper Mark Carter offer elegant accommodations. The Carter
House, a redwood neo-Victorian, has seven guest rooms, four of
which have private baths. All the rooms are spacious and furnished
tastefully. It is a 3-floor, 20-room that looks old but is actually a
new structure. The 20 rooms are furnished in contemporary style.
All have private baths. Rates at both establishments are moderate
to expensive. The Carter House is at 1033 Third Street, Eureka, CA
95501. 707/445-1390. The Hotel Carter is at 301 L Street, Eureka,
CA 95501. 707/444-8062.

✪ *Old Town Bed and Breakfast Inn.* Once the residence of lumber baron William Carson, this former mill is now a cute and cozy
inn. The five rooms are decorated with antiques. Three have
private baths. Inexpensive. 1521 Third Street, Eureka, CA 95501.
707/445-3951.

✪ *A Weaver's Inn.* This century-old inn has four comfortable
rooms (two share a bath), but the main attractions are the Japanese gardens, soaking tub, and the weaving/fiber art studio. Moderate. 1440 B Street, Eureka, CA 95501. 707/443-8119.

Eureka: Fine Dining

✪ *Carter House*. Californian cuisine served in a romantic Victorian setting. Expensive. 1033 Third Street. 707/444-8062.

✪ *Lazio's*. The finest seafood restaurant in the area. Moderate. First and C streets. 707/443-9717.

✪ *Samoa Cookhouse*. The ambiance leaves a little to be desired, but this funky local hangout serves interesting family-style meals at long wooden tables. Inexpensive. Across Samoa Bridge off Highway 1 on the Samoa Road. 707/442-1659.

Ferndale: Romantic Lodging

✪ *The Gingerbread Mansion*. This magnificent turreted mansion blends Queen Anne and Eastlake architecture into a fairy-tale palace. There are nine large guest rooms, each decorated individually with antiques and all with private baths. Two of the rooms have "his and her" clawfoot bathtubs. Moderate. 400 Berding Street, Ferndale, CA 95536. 707/786-4000.

Ferndale: Fine Dining

✪ *Sunset Grille*. The grilled fish and meats are excellent at this casual dining spot. Moderate. 703 South Fortune Boulevard, in Fortuna (30 minutes from Ferndale). 707/725-1156.

Fort Bragg: Romantic Lodging

✪ *Blue Rose Inn*. There are five beautiful rooms in this lovely Cape Cod Victorian inn next to what innkeeper Anne Samas calls "the best garden in town." The rooms are bright and airy. Inexpensive. 520 North Main Street, Fort Bragg, CA 95437. 707/964-3477.

❁ *Country Inn.* There are eight comfortable rooms in this century-old home whose interior is paneled in redwood. All the rooms have contemporary furnishings and private baths. Moderate. 632 North Main Street, Fort Bragg, CA 95437. 707/964-3737.

❁ *The Grey Whale Inn.* This landmark building served as a hospital until the 1970s, when it was spruced up and converted into a lovely bed-and-breakfast. There are 14 rooms, all with private baths and each individually decorated. Moderate. 615 North Main Street, Fort Bragg, CA 95437. 707/964-0640.

❁ *Noyo River Lodge.* Overlooking the marina, this century-old redwood Victorian inn offers 13 rooms, furnished with antiques, fireplaces, and, in some rooms, double soaking tubs. Moderate/expensive. 500 Casa del Noyo Drive, Fort Bragg, CA 95437. 707/964-8045.

❁ *Pudding Creek Inn.* The two century-old Victorian buildings are joined by an enclosed garden court, giving the guests a lovely place for breakfast and quiet moments. The 10 rooms are cozy and furnished with collectibles. Moderate. 700 North Main Street, Fort Bragg, CA 95437. 707/964-9529.

Fort Bragg: Fine Dining

❁ *The Restaurant.* It's an art gallery as well as a dining room serving fine Californian cuisine. Moderate. 418 North Main Street. 707/964-9800.

❁ *The Wharf.* Good seafood and steaks, whether you dine indoors or outside where you will have a great view of the fishing fleet and the harbor. Moderate. 780 North Harbor Drive. 707/964-4283.

Garberville: Romantic Lodging

✪ *Benbow Inn.* The elegant Tudor Inn has been visited by Eleanor Roosevelt, Charles Laughton, and other celebrities seeking the serenity and beauty of the Redwood Empire. The 55 rooms are comfortable, and decorated with art, antiques, and collectibles. The inn is on the Eel River and is near the Avenue of the Giants. Moderate/expensive. 445 Lake Benbow Drive, Garberville, CA 95440. 707/923-2124.

Garberville: Fine Dining

✪ *The Benbow Inn.* Californian cuisine, featuring fresh meat and seafood of the season served in a cozy wood-paneled room with a fireplace. Expensive. 445 Lake Benbow Drive. 707/923-2124.

✪ *Woodrose Cafe.* Fresh seafood and fine pastas in a casual setting. Moderate. 911 Redwood Drive. 707/923-3191.

Gualala: Romantic Lodging

✪ *Old Milano Hotel.* Built as a Victorian pub next to the rail line and modernized to hide its past, this lovely inn offers seven guest rooms in the main house and two more in a cottage and a converted caboose. The furnishings are a mixture of antiques, from elegant to comfortable. Three of the rooms have private baths. Moderate. 38300 Highway 1, Gualala, CA 95445. 707/884-3256.

✪ *St. Orres.* This 1920s hotel has been renovated in a stunning inn, featuring twin domed towers, an entryway graced by art nouveau and Edwardian antiques, and a spare-no-expense use of redwood and glass inside and out. There are eight rooms in the main house, most of which share his and her baths, and nine cottages. The rooms are luxurious. Moderate. 36601 Highway 1 South, Gualala, CA 95445. 707/884-3303.

✪ *Whale Watch Inn.* There are 18 rooms in this contemporary inn built on the coast south of Mendocino. The inn is on a bluff, and the rooms offer fantastic views of the sea (and the whales from December through March). The furnishings are contemporary. Expensive. 35100 Highway 1, Gualala, CA 95445. 707/883-3667.

Gualala: Fine Dining

✪ *Old Milano.* Country-style meals served in the inn. 38300 Highway 1. 707/884-3256.

✪ *St. Orres.* This excellent restaurant serves a creative menu, featuring fine dinners at a fixed price. This may be the best restaurant north of San Francisco. 36601 Highway 1 South. 707/884-3335.

Inverness: Romantic Lodging

✪ *Blackthorne Inn.* This lovely inn is a treehouse fantasyland of wooden staircases, decks, a tower, and a bridgeway. The most romantic room is Eagles Nest, located in an octagonal, glass-walled tower. The five guest rooms are furnished with antiques and reproduction pieces and share baths. Moderate/expensive. 266 Vallejo, P.O. Box 712, Inverness, CA 94937. 415/663-8621.

Inverness: Fine Dining

✪ *Manka's.* Czech cuisine is a surprise, but the food is excellent. The dining room is romantic, with a fireplace and lovely decor. Moderate. 30 Calendar Way. 415/669-1034.

Inverness Park: Romantic Lodging

✪ *Holly Tree Inn.* Just a mile from Point Reyes National Seashore, this lodge offers four nicely decorated rooms and a new cottage a short walk away on the 19-acre estate. The furnishings are country antiques. Moderate. The inn is at 3 Silverhill Road in Inverness Park, but the mailing address is P.O. Box 642, Point Reyes Station, CA 94956. 415/663-1554.

Jenner: Romantic Lodging

✪ *Timber Cove Inn.* The 49 luxury rooms have wonderful views of the cove, and about half have fireplaces and hot tubs. Expensive. 2178 North Highway 1 (about 3 miles north of Fort Ross), Jenner, CA 95450. 707/847-3231.

✪ *Timberhill Ranch.* One of the most beautiful and luxurious resorts on the north coast, this elegant country inn offers 10 secluded cottages, all very spacious and romantic. The rooms have fireplaces and antique furnishings. Facilities include a pool and jacuzzi surrounded by a forest, tennis courts, and a fantastic restaurant. Room rates include breakfast and six-course dinner. Expensive. 35755 Hauser Bridge Road, Cazadero, CA 95421. 707/847-3258.

Jenner: Fine Dining

✪ *River's End.* The cuisine is a surprise. It's German, and the venison and seafood are exceptional. Moderate. Highway 1 north of Jenner. 707/865-2484.

Mill Valley: Romantic Lodging

✪ *Mountain Home Inn.* Located on a ridge overlooking Muir Woods, this elegant mountain lodge of redwood, glass, and cedar has 10 guest rooms, all with private baths and stunning views.

Each room is comfortable and comes with a private bath and a bottle of champagne. Moderate. 810 Panoramic Highway, Mill Valley, CA 94941. 415/381-9000.

Mill Valley: Fine Dining

✪ *Mountain Home Inn.* Californian cuisine with continental accents, featuring mostly seafoods and pastas. The dining room is lovely. Try the outdoor deck in nice weather. Moderate. 810 Panoramic Highway. 415/381-9000.

Muir Beach: Romantic Lodging

✪ *The Pelican Inn.* The Tudor-style inn is home to an English-style pub as well as six guest rooms. The rooms are comfortable and furnished with English antiques, canopy beds, and private baths. Moderate. Highway 1, Muir Beach, CA 94965. 415/383-6000.

Muir Beach: Fine Dining

✪ *The Pelican Inn.* Fish and chips and Yorkshire pudding make this English-style pub a special place. Moderate. Highway 1. 415/383-6005.

Point Reyes Station: Romantic Lodging

✪ *Jasmine Cottage.* Originally the carriage house for the 1878 schoolhouse, this lovely little cottage offers one room, with a fireplace and antique furnishings. Moderate/expensive. P.O. Box 56, Point Reyes Station, CA 94956. 415/663-1166.

Point Reyes Station: Fine Dining

✪ *Chez Madeline.* Good French cuisine served in a romantic setting. The seafood dishes are the best here. Expensive. Highway 1, Point Reyes. 415/663-9177.

Sausalito: Romantic Lodging

❂ *Casa Madrona Hotel.* There are 34 antique-filled rooms in this majestic century-old Victorian hotel built by a lumber baron. Expensive. 801 Bridgeway, Sausalito, CA 94965. 415/332-0502.

❂ *Sausalito Hotel.* This hotel next to the ferry dock offers fantastic views of the bay and San Francisco as well as 15 rooms furnished with high-quality antiques. Expensive. 16 El Portal, Sausalito, CA 94965. 415/332-4155.

Sausalito: Fine Dining

❂ *Casa Madrona.* This hotel dining room serves excellent American fare (rare in these parts). The Sunday brunch is also a hit. Moderate. 801 Bridgeway. 415/331-5888.

❂ *Ondine.* Elegant dining room, fantastic views of the bay and superb continental cuisine. The specialty is pheasant Vladimir with vodka and sour cream sauce, but the fresh seafood is also excellent. Expensive. 558 Bridgeway. 415/332-0791.

❂ *Scoma's.* This restaurant is almost too cute: flowers in little boxes, lovely antiques, and a great view of the bay. The Italian seafood, even without the lovely surroundings, is the attraction. Moderate. 588 Bridgeway. 415/332-9551.

Central Coast, by City:
Romantic Lodging and Fine Dining

Big Sur: Romantic Lodging

❂ *Ventana Inn.* This luxury resort is located on a 240-acre ranch up in the mountains overlooking the Pacific Coast. The resort is popular with such stars as Henry Winkler and Goldie Hawn, who like its location and sense of privacy. The 59 rooms are in 12 contemporary lodges. The decor can best be called rustic yet elegant. The rooms are spacious and have terraces, dressing rooms, and wicker furnishings. Facilities include two heated pools and a Japanese bath (with three sections: one for each sex and one for both where clothing is an option). Expensive. Highway 1, Big Sur, CA 93920. 408/667-2331 and 800/628-6500 nationwide.

Big Sur: Fine Dining

✪ *Ventana Inn.* Californian cuisine served in a rustic wood-and-stone hillside dining room. Expensive. Highway 1. 408/667-2331.

Cambria: Romantic Lodging

✪ *Blue Whale Inn.* This contemporary Cape Cod inn has six rooms, all furnished with Victorian antiques. Most of the rooms have ocean views and fireplaces. Expensive. 6736 Moonstone Beach Drive, Cambria, CA 93428. 805/927-4647.

✪ *J. Patrick House.* This cute log cabin and the cedar-shingled lodge behind it offer eight cozy rooms, all with antiques, fireplaces, and private baths. Moderate. 2990 Burton Drive, Cambria, CA 93428. 805/927-3812.

✪ *Olallieberry Inn.* There are six rooms in this beautiful 1873 Greek Revival mansion. The rooms have antique decor and fireplaces. Moderate. 2476 Main Street, Cambria, CA 93428. 805/927-3222.

Cambria: Fine Dining

✪ *Brambles Dinner House.* The specialty of the house is seafood, particularly the salmon cooked over an oak fire, at this popular restaurant. Moderate. 4005 Burton Drive. 805/927-4716.

✪ *Hamlet at Moonstone Gardens.* We like the name and the fact that the dining room is surrounded by a plant nursery. The cuisine ranges from burgers to excellent fish dishes. Moderate. Highway 1. 805/927-3535.

Monterey: Romantic Lodging

✪ *Hotel Pacific.* This charming adobe-style hotel has 104 suites, all large and nicely decorated. Expensive. 300 Pacific Street, Monterey, CA 93940. 408/373-5700; and 800/554-5542 in California, 800/225-2903 elsewhere in the United States.

✪ *Hyatt Regency.* This large and modern resort offers 575 rooms, a golf course, 6 tennis courts, 2 pools, an exercise room and course, and a host of other activities. Expensive. 1 Old Golf Course Road, Monterey, CA 93940. 408/372-1234.

✪ *Jabberwock.* The theme is Alice in Wonderland in this majestic inn. Antiques, beautiful gardens, and a whimsical style make this a special place. Moderate/expensive. 598 Laine Street, Monterey, CA 93940. 408/372-4777.

✪ *Monterey Plaza.* Look out your window at the waterfront and watch the otters play in this comfortable hotel that blends mission and oriental decor. There are 290 spacious, well-appointed rooms. Expensive. 400 Cannery Row, Monterey, CA 93940. 408/646-1700; and 800/334-3999 in California, 800/631-1339 elsewhere in the United States.

✪ *Old Monterey Inn.* Surrounded by gardens and located in a quiet section of Monterey, this English Tudor inn has nine elegant rooms and a cottage, all with private baths. Expensive. 500 Martin Street, Monterey, CA 93940. 408/375-8284.

✿ *Spindrift Inn.* Small and elegant, this hotel on Cannery Row has 41 huge rooms with canopied beds and fireplaces. Expensive. 652 Cannery Row, Monterey, CA 93940. 408/646-8900; and 800/841-1879 in California, 800/225-2901 elsewhere in the United States.

Monterey: Fine Dining

✿ *Abalonetti.* This Fisherman's Wharf spot is very casual. The seafood is sensational. Try the fresh fish, shellfish, or shrimp and don't miss the cioppino (it's similar to bouillabaisse) and the chowders. Inexpensive. 57 Fisherman's Wharf. 408/375-5941.

✿ *Fresh Cream.* Creative Californian cuisine in a charming dining room. Try the fresh quail or squab from the nearby game farms. Expensive. 100 Pacific Street. 408/375-9798.

✿ *Neil de Vaughn's.* Seafood and fondue at this landmark on Cannery Row. Expensive. 654 Cannery Row. 408/372-2141.

✿ *The Old House in Monterey.* Fine continental cuisine served in an 1840 adobe house. Expensive. 500 Hartnell Street. 408/373-3737.

✿ *Old Monterey Cafe.* Daylong breakfast and brunch fare in a casual setting. Inexpensive. 489 Alvarado Street. 408/646-1021.

✿ *Sancho Panza.* Excellent Mexican dishes with a setting to match in this 150-year-old adobe house. Inexpensive. 590 Calle Principal. 408/375-0095.

✿ *Sardine Factory.* Located in one of the processing plants on Cannery Row, this Gay '90s–theme restaurant serves excellent Italian seafood. Expensive. 701 Wave Street. 408/373-3775.

✪ *Steinbeck Lobster Grotto.* Excellent seafood and fish soups with great views of the ocean. Moderate. 720 Cannery Row. 408/373-1884.

✪ *Whaling Station Inn.* Elegant yet rustic, this dining room serves the best mesquite-grilled fish and meat on the peninsula. Expensive. 763 Wave Street. 408/373-3778.

Morro Bay: Romantic Lodging

✪ *The Inn at Morro Bay.* There are 96 rooms at this spacious resort with a pool, 18-hole golf course, putting green, and driving range. The rooms are spacious and nicely furnished. Expensive. 19 Country Club Road, Morro Bay, CA 93442. 805/772-5651 and 800/321-9566 nationwide.

Morro Bay: Fine Dining

✪ *Dorn's.* Cute and casual cafe atmosphere with fine seafood. Try the abalone. The restaurant overlooks the harbor and main square. Moderate. 801 Market Street. 805/772-4415.

Pacific Grove: Romantic Lodging

✪ *Gosby House.* Sharing ownership with the Green Gables, this inn started life a century ago and slowly expanded, with its original owner adding a tower, bay windows, and other amenities. There are 22 rooms, all but two of which have a private bath. The rooms are cozy and nicely furnished. Moderate/expensive. 643 Lighthouse Avenue, Pacific Grove, CA 93950. 408/375-1287.

✪ *Green Gables.* This small but elegant Queen Anne inn overlooks the bay and has 11 cozy rooms, most with views of the water. Six of the rooms are in the mansion, the other five are in the adjacent cottage. Moderate/expensive. 104 Fifth Street, Pacific Grove, CA 93950. 408/375-2095.

✿ *House of Seven Gables Inn.* Overlooking Monterey Bay, this century-old mansion was one of a number built on the cliff in the late 1800s. There are 14 guest rooms, decorated in an eclectic mix of antiques from the Victorian era. All the rooms have private baths. Moderate/expensive. 555 Ocean View Boulevard, Pacific Grove, CA 93950. 408/372-4341.

✿ *The Martine Inn.* Built in 1899 as a Victorian and later re-modeled into a Mediterranean-style villa (somehow, it works), this lovely 19-room inn overlooks Monterey Bay and the frolicking otters and seals. The furnishings are exquisite antiques, ranging from Oriental pieces to Chippendale to Art Deco. Thirteen rooms have fireplaces, most have ocean views, and all have private baths. Moderate/expensive. 255 Ocean View Boulevard, Pacific Grove, CA 93950. 408/373-3388.

Pacific Grove: Fine Dining

✿ *Fish and Basil.* Fresh seafood and pastas are excellent at this lovely gardenlike restaurant. Moderate. 105 Ocean View Boulevard. 408/649-0707.

✿ *Gernot's Victorian House.* Fine Californian-French cuisine served in the elegant Victorian Hart Mansion. Expensive. 649 Lighthouse Avenue. 408/646-1477.

✿ *Old Bath House.* The setting is romantic—a bathhouse on the water at Lovers Point. The cuisine is continental—the fresh seafood is the best choice. Expensive. 620 Ocean View Boulevard. 408/375-5195.

Pebble Beach: Romantic Lodging

✿ *The Inn at Spanish Bay.* More casual than its sister The Lodge at Pebble Beach, this sprawling 270-room resort on the shore on

17-Mile Drive offers magnificent views and luxurious rooms. Facilities include a pool and tennis courts, and guests may use the facilities at The Lodge at Pebble Beach. Expensive. Box 1418, 2700 17-Mile Drive, Pebble Beach, CA 93953. 408/647-7500 and 800/654-9300 nationwide.

✿ *The Lodge at Pebble Beach.* Formal, luxurious, and world famous since 1916, this refined resort offers 161 elegant rooms. Facilities include golf, tennis, pool, health spa, and an equestrian center. Expensive. Box 1418, 17-Mile Drive, Pebble Beach, CA 93953. 408/624-3811 and 800/654-9300 nationwide.

Pebble Beach: Fine Dining

✿ *The Bay Club.* Creative continental dining at this restaurant in the Inn at Spanish Bay. Expensive. 2700 17-Mile Drive. 408/654-7500.

✿ *Club XIX.* Outstanding French dishes, elegant setting, and a cafe atmosphere in this room at The Lodge at Pebble Beach. 17-Mile Drive, three miles north of Carmel. Expensive. 408/624-3811.

✿ *The Dunes.* Californian cuisine in a casual setting in this room at the Inn at Spanish Bay. Eat outside if you can. Moderate. 2700 17-Mile Drive. 408/654-7500.

San Luis Obispo: Romantic Lodging

✿ *Madonna Inn.* This fantasyland castle has 109 rooms, all decorated in different fantasy themes, ranging from Cave Man to Big Game Hunter to the more feminine Victorian Gardens and the all-pink honeymoon suite called the Love Nest. Moderate to expensive, depending on your fantasy. Note: The more popular rooms book up weeks ahead, and the entire hotel is almost always filled.

If you have particular fantasies that need fulfilling, book months ahead. 100 Madonna Road, San Luis Obispo, CA 93401. 805/543-3000.

For more information on other attractions, lodging, and restaurants on the coast, see the sections on Carmel, Mendocino, and Santa Barbara in Chapter One.

Chapter Four

✦

The Desert Empire

From the top of San Jacinto Mountain, the Coachella Valley below seems to stretch forever. The gold and white colors of the expanses of sand are broken by only two things: the mountain ranges that separate one desert valley from the next, and sprawling, irregular squares of dark green.

As magical as the endless miles of golden sands are, the real attractions in the Desert Empire are in a synthetic oasis. The names are magic around the world: Palm Desert, Palm Springs, and Rancho Mirage. They have come to symbolize wealth, elegance, golf, tennis, and other diversions of the rich.

North of the playground of the stars is a desert that is a sharp contrast to these fabled resorts. The Mojave Desert is a high desert, with elevations of from 3,000 feet up to a mile above sea level. This desert is cooler than that of the Coachella Valley. During the winter, snow occasionally falls in the Mojave. A century ago this high desert attracted miners, a few of which struck it rich when they found gold and silver in the hills. The mother lode in these hills isn't precious metals anymore; the treasure is some of the most beautiful and desolate scenery on earth.

In the northeast corner of the Mojave are ancient lake beds that have become famous because of their name: Death Valley. The name is misleading, for the valley is filled with color of all kinds—more than 1,000 species of plants including 21 found nowhere else in the world.

Death Valley's attractions include those of dreams, both broken and fulfilled. There is the ghost town of Calico, which is reborn with arts festivals, and the unfinished mansion known as Scotty's castle. And there is an opera house, in a town with a population of 2, that one dreamer turned into a popular playhouse.

In the desert, man's presence seems a tenuous thing, something tolerated for now by the surrounding sands. That's understandable, for nothing remains the same in the desert. The colors of soil and mountain are everchanging. First gold, then a grayish white that quickly fades to green with a hint of lavender. Even the plants play a role in this cycle of change. For most of the year the scrub bushes—creosote, Joshua tree, yucca, saguaro, indigobush—look so dry and dead that a stiff wind will send them on their way. With winter rains they come alive with an explosion of life and color. And from the empty sands comes another surprise, carpets of white primroses and yellow marigolds.

It's a surprise to visitors, for they come with a vision of a desert that doesn't include any images of life. That's very wrong, for these deserts are filled with surprises.

❂ KINGDOM OF THE SUN—PALM SPRINGS AND THE COACHELLA VALLEY

The center of the desert resorts is Palm Springs, which has been dubbed the "Playground of the Stars" as well as the "Golf Capital of the World." While Palm Springs is no longer the chic address in

✪ The dramatic landscape of the Joshua Tree National Monument. (Courtesy of the Palm Springs Desert Resorts Convention and Visitors Bureau)

the Coachella Valley (Palm Desert and Rancho Mirage can claim supremacy), it is still the beautiful kingdom of recreation. Consider these numbers: 7,500 swimming pools, more than 600 tennis courts, and at least 80 golf courses and miles of hiking and riding trails.

Humphrey Bogart, Bob Hope, Frank Sinatra, Esther Williams, and other luminaries made this desert resort world famous. What attracted these stars was the climate: an average daytime high of 88 degrees and low of 55, plus 350 days of sunshine each year.

The first resorts that attracted Hollywood figures were followed by bigger, ever more lavish spas. In time, Palm Springs became a sprawling city, and just one of a series of desert towns that are a surprising mixture of elegant resorts and pricey boutiques located next to middle-class housing developments and shopping centers.

For shoppers, the finest shops are in Palm Springs and Palm Desert. In Palm Springs, the main shopping district is along South and North Palm Canyon Drive and the adjacent Indian Avenue, between Ramon Road and Alejo Road. These shops are interesting, and offer a wide variety of jewelry, clothing, art, and other nice items, but you get the feeling that the district isn't as chic as it may have been in the past. There are too many souvenir and T-shirt shops among the fashionable stores, and they mar the elegant image.

This feeling was confirmed when we visited El Paseo, the very chic and very expensive shopping district in Palm Desert. This lovely boulevard is one block south and east of the intersection of highways 111 and 74. Here we found finer shops and a more genteel setting than the busy commercial strip in Palm Springs. Among the better stores are The Campayré Fine Jewelry (73-770 El Paseo), designer jewelry and china; the Diane Freis Boutique (73-111 El Paseo), designer dresses; Ted Land (73-725 El Paseo), elegant shoes and handbags; Greta (73-130 El Paseo), designer clothing; and Edith Morré Fashions (73-690 El Paseo), designer apparel. Even if they are beyond your budget (they were way beyond our bank account), it's still fun to look.

If it's too warm to stroll these streets, visit the posh Palm Desert Town Center, an air-conditioned mall with upscale shops, five major department stores, theaters, restaurants, and an ice rink. It's at highways 74 and 111.

After visiting these two shopping districts, it would be easy to believe that these desert resorts are nothing but vast country clubs with shops. Not true. The McCallum Theatre in Palm Springs is a showcase for top performing artists, and art, film, jazz, and Dixieland are celebrated in huge festivals during the year.

More art can be viewed at the Aerie Sculpture Garden in Palm Desert, the Coachella Valley Museum in Indio, and the Edward-Dean Museum of Decorative Arts (from the seventeenth and eighteenth centuries) in Cherry Valley.

The other major attraction in this desert is found all around you. The desert and the mountains may look barren, but they are filled with a wide variety of plant and animal life. All it requires to discover is a will strong enough to tear you away from the brilliantly green fairways and inviting swimming pools.

Start by taking the aerial tramway from Tramway Drive off Highway 111 north of Palm Springs. There you can ride an aerial car from the desert floor up to 8,516 feet up the side of the 10,831-foot Mt. San Jacinto. The ascent takes 20 minutes, and the view from the state park at the top can be spectacular, if the air is clear of haze. During the winter, you can take the tramway to the mountain and go cross-country skiing on the park's miles of trails.

Nature isn't ignored back on the valley floor. The Coachella Valley Preserve, on Thousand Palms Canyon Road 2 miles east of Ramon Road, is a spectacular palm-shaded oasis surrounded by a

13,000-acre preserve with crystal springs, bluffs, and sand dunes. The preserve's hiking trails have signs that are informative and make the hike more interesting.

The Living Desert (47-900 Portola Avenue) in Palm Desert, is a 1,200-acre desert interpretive center. Exotic birds and animals as well as botanical gardens and nature trails make this a special place. More than 2,000 varieties of cacti, succulents, and other desert plants can be found at Moorten's Botanical Garden (1701 South Palm Canyon Drive) in Palm Springs.

Putting the present and the past of the desert into perspective is the Palm Springs Desert Museum, west of the Desert Fashion Plaza (101 Museum Drive) in Palm Springs. Exhibits, a theater, and a cultural center explore the history of the Aqua Caliente Indians who inhabit the valley and first discovered what they called the "miracle healing waters." For more information on the valley's interesting history, visit the Village Green Heritage Center, which is made up of two nineteenth-century homes. The museum (221 and 223 Palm Canyon Drive South in Palm Springs) houses the collection of the Palm Springs Historical Society.

Even more wonders of history and nature are outside of the resorts. The Indian Canyons at the south end of Palm Canyon Drive 5 miles from town is an Indian reservation where the ancient stone houses have been preserved in a wilderness of trees and palms and towering cliffs. The Joshua Tree National Monument on Highway 62 north of Interstate 10 is a 467,000-acre park filled with thousands of the 40-foot-tall cactus. Along the way to this park you will pass Big Morongo Wildlife Preserve, an oasis with a wide variety of animal and plant life.

Every spring, if there is enough rainfall, the greatest show in the desert is the explosion of gaily colored wildflowers at Joshua Tree. Another colorful attraction at Joshua Tree is the Desert Queen Ranch, a deserted ranch where the lifestyle of the 1880s has been well preserved. Here you can see an old stamp mill, Indian ruins, an adobe barn, and structures built later by a quaint old character called William Keys. Guided trips to the ranch are scheduled from February through Memorial Day and mid-October to mid-December. Sign up at the park visitors center.

Other attractions at Joshua Tree include the Lost Palms oasis, a beautiful sanctuary that is home to a number of bird species and palms, and Hidden Valley, a jumbled maze of rock that legend says was a hideout for rustlers. The Lost Palms oasis is a 4-mile hike from the visitors center at the Cottonwood Springs entrance, just north of Interstate 10. Hidden Valley is a few miles in from the Joshua Tree entrance to the monument.

The mountains surrounding the Coachella Valley offer a stunning backdrop to the beauty of the desert floor. The colors of the mountainside are constantly changing because of the passing clouds and sunlight. In winter, the San Jacinto Mountains are often coated with a topping of white from snow storms. From your chaise at poolside, it's a spectacular sight, even though it seems a world away.

✪ MOJAVE DESERT AND DEATH VALLEY

Rugged mountains, deep and mysterious canyons, and an ocean of sand make the Mojave Desert a region of enchanting beauty. The landscape is eerie, like something created in a dream. Here are canyons of dramatic rocks and colors, ghost towns, and eerie reminders of the past. Touring it requires a curiosity. The Mojave and Death Valley are not something to speed through at 60 miles an hour. The landscape begs you to stop and take a closer look, to see the beauty that others once derided as the badlands.

The Mojave Desert is crisscrossed by several major highways that take you to the top attractions in this dramatic region.

Interstate 15, the major road from Los Angeles, exits the San Bernadino National Forest and heads north past Victorville and the Roy Rogers and Dale Evans Museum honoring those two western stars and continues to Barstow. This mining town has the Desert Information Center (831 Barstow Road) which has exhibits, maps, and other information about the Mojave. Get precise directions at the center for those sights you wish to visit.

Eight miles north of Barstow is Rainbow Basin, a region where something violent happened eons ago. The rocks are twisted into tortured shapes, and the colors shift from reds to greens to blacks and whites, as if the earth couldn't make up its mind. The gulleys and ravines hold their own mysteries, the fossilized skeletons of animals that lived millions of years ago. You can look at these fossils, but don't take them. It's against federal law.

North of Barstow on Ghost Town Road, 3 miles north of Interstate 15, is Calico, a ghost town that had about 3,500 residents during the silver boom in the 1880s. The town has been restored recently, and visitors can tour it and the tunnels of the Silver King Mine.

These early miners were not the first settlers in this barren valley, not by thousands of years. Thousands of scrapers, picks, saws, and other tools dating back to 200,000 years ago have been found at the Calico Early Man Archeological Site on U.S. 15, 15 miles north of Barstow. Dr. Louis Leakey, the famed archeologist, was director of this dig for nine years until his death in 1972.

Another 23 miles north on U.S. 15 is Afton Valley, a deep gorge carved by the Mojave River. After viewing this lush valley, continue on Interstate 15 until you come to Baker.

At Baker, turn south on the Kelbaker Road to a majestic dune world. Forty-two miles south (7 miles beyond the town of Kelso) are the Kelso Dunes, a magnificent ocean of wind-sculpted sand.

The dunes cover more than 70 square miles and can reach about 500 feet in height.

Return to Baker and head north on Highway 127 to Death Valley. It's an 84-mile drive to Death Valley Junction, a small (population 2) crossroads where the major attraction isn't the desert. It's the Marta Becket's Amargosa Opera House. Becket, a New York dancer, first saw the town in 1964 and became stranded in it with a flat tire three years later. Enchanted with the boarded-up theater, Becket bought it, refurbished it (complete with a fantastic trompe l'oeil painting of an audience), and began presenting a show of mime, ballet, and melodrama. The shows are often sold out.

After the opera house, drive north on Highway 190 first to Zabriskie Point, a lookout with a nice view of the valley, and then to Highway 178, where you turn south and drive 13 miles to Dante's View, another lookout. This lookout is more than a mile above sea level, and offers stunning views of the whole valley.

Return to Highway 190 and turn north for the Death Valley National Monument Visitors Center and Museum at Furnace Creek. The center has exhibits, maps, and other information about the national park.

Just north of the Center is the Borax Museum (remember the old "20-mule-team Borax" commercials in the show "Death Valley Days," hosted by Ronald Reagan?). The ruins of the Harmony Borax Works are 2 miles north of the museum.

Take the North Highway about 50 miles north to Scotty's Castle, an unfinished Moorish dream started by Walter Scott, a cowboy who starred in Buffalo Bill's Wild West Show. Scott never finished his mansion when the stock market crashed in 1929. Today, the partially complete castle is furnished with fine rugs, an organ, antiques, and works of art. It's out of place in the desert, and perhaps that makes it even more special. One man's dream, in a landscape that few could ever dream existed.

Throughout your tour of Death Valley, remember that the lure of the region is not the castle or the borax works or the other man-made attractions. It's the splendid desolation of this land burdened by such a horrible name. Death came all too easily to the first pioneers trying to cross this inhospitable region. The name curse left by them rejects the awesome beauty that this desert can show. Show, that is, to those who take time to look.

✿ FOR MORE INFORMATION

Palm Springs and the Coachella Valley

Palm Springs Desert Resorts Convention and Visitors Bureau. Atrium Design Centre, 69-930 Highway 111, Suite 201, Rancho Mirage, 92270. 619/770-9000.

Mojave Desert and Death Valley

Death Valley Chamber of Commerce. 2 Post Office Row, Tecopa, CA 92389. 619/852-4524.

Death Valley National Monument. Death Valley, CA 92328. 619/786-2331.

Mojave Chamber of Commerce. 15836 Sierra Highway, Mojave, CA 93501. 805/824-2481.

✿ WHERE AND WHEN

Palm Springs and the Coachella Valley

Aerie Sculpture Garden. 71-255 Aerie Drive, Palm Desert. By appointment only September through May. 619/568-6366.

Big Morongo Wildlife Reserve. East Drive in Morongo Valley. Open 7:30 AM to sunset Wednesday through Sunday. 619/363-7190.

Coachella Valley Museum. 82-616 Miles Avenue, Indio. 619/342-6651.

Coachella Valley Preserve. Thousand Palms Canyon Road. Open daily dawn to dusk. 619/343-1234.

Edward-Dean Museum of Decorative Arts. 9401 Oak Glen Road, Cherry Valley. Open 1 PM to 4:30 PM Tuesday through Friday, 10 AM to 4:30 PM Saturday and Sunday, closed Monday and August. 714/845-2626.

Indian Canyons. South Palm Canyon Drive, Palm Springs. Open daily September through June. 619/325-5673.

Joshua Tree National Monument. Route 62. Open 24 hours. 619/367-7511.

Living Desert. 47-900 Portola Drive, Palm Desert. Open 9 AM to 5 PM daily; closed mid-June through August. 619/346-5694.

McCallum Theatre for the Performing Arts. 73-000 Fred Waring Drive, Palm Desert. Shows September through July. 619/346-6505.

Moorten Botanical Garden. 1701 South Palm Canyon Drive, Palm Springs. Open 9 AM to 4:30 PM daily. 619/327-6555.

Palm Springs Aerial Tramway. Tramway Drive. Open 10 AM to 8 PM weekdays, 8 AM to 8 PM (9 PM in the summer) weekends and holidays. 619/325-4227.

Palm Springs Desert Museum. 101 Museum Drive, Palm Springs. Open 10 AM to 4 PM Tuesday through Friday, 10 AM to 5 PM weekends. 619/325-0189.

Village Green Heritage Center. 221-223 South Palm Canyon Drive, Palm Springs. Hours vary. Call 619/323-8297.

Mojave Desert and Death Valley

Calico Early Man Archeological Site. Minneola Road 3 miles north of Interstate 15. Open 8 AM to 4:30 PM Wednesday through Sunday. 619/256-3591.

Calico Ghost Town. Ghost Town Road, off Interstate 15. Open 9 AM to 5 PM daily. 619/254-2122.

Death Valley Visitors Center. Highway 190. Open 8 AM to 8 PM daily. 619/786-2331.

Desert Information Center. 831 Barstow Road, Barstow. Open 9 AM to 5 PM daily. 619/256-8617.

Marta Becket's Amargosa Opera House. Death Valley Junction. Performances November through April at 8:15 PM Friday, Saturday, and Monday; May through October at 8:15 PM Saturday. 619/852-4316.

Roy Rogers and Dale Evans Museum. Mojave Narrows Park, 15650 Seneca Road. Open 9 AM to 5 PM daily. 619/243-4547.

Scotty's Castle. North Highway 190. Open 7 AM to 6 PM daily. 619/786-2331.

✪ ROMANTIC RETREATS

These two desert trips offer distinctly different levels of accommodations. Palm Springs and its sister communities are filled with lavish resorts and hotels. The Mojave Desert and Death Valley, obviously, offer fewer and less elegant accommodations.

Here are our favorites, but first an explanation of how we break down our cost categories:

One night in a hotel, resort, or inn for two:

Inexpensive	Less than $75
Moderate	$75 to $125
Expensive	More than $125

Dinner for two (drinks not included):

Inexpensive	Less than $25
Moderate	$25 to $60
Expensive	More than $60

Palm Springs: Romantic Lodging

✪ *Hyatt Grand Champions.* This sprawling resort seems to have every recreation outlet possible: two 18-hole golf courses, 12 tennis courts, a putting green and driving range, lawn games, bicycles, four heated pools, exercise room, and full-service health spa. The 321 rooms are large and luxurious. Twenty Italian-style villas offer elaborate landscaping, privacy, and 24-hour butler service. Expensive. 44-600 Indian Wells Lane, Indians Wells, CA 92210. 619/341-1000.

✪ *Ingleside Inn.* The 29 spacious rooms in this small Spanish-style inn are furnished with antiques and a whirlpool. Expensive. 200 West Ramon Road, Palm Springs, CA 92264. 619/325-0046; and 800/826-4162 in California, 800/772-6655 elsewhere in the United States.

✪ *La Mancha Private Pool Villas and Court Club.* There are 54 huge villas and 7 minisuites at this private retreat only a few blocks from the heart of Palm Springs. The villas have a full kitchen, and most have a private pool. Some have fireplaces and one has a private tennis court. Facilities include tennis, two pools, and lawn games. Expensive. 444 North Avenida Cabilleros, Palm Springs, CA 92263. 619/323-1773; and 800/255-1773 in California, 800/854-1298 elsewhere in the United States.

✪ *Marriott's Desert Springs Resort and Spa.* This luxurious 891-room resort has it all: two 18-hole golf courses, a European spa, 16 tennis courts, beautiful rooms, and transport around the resort on boats cruising a series of canals. Expensive. 74855 Country Club Drive, Palm Desert, CA 92260. 619/341-2211 and 800/228-9290 nationwide.

✪ *Mira Loma Hotel.* Cozy and cute, with 12 rooms furnished in art deco style and furnishings. Inexpensive. 1420 North Indian Avenue, Palms Springs, CA 92263. 619/320-1178.

✪ *La Quinta Hotel Golf and Tennis Resort.* Large and elegant, this 641-room resort has two 18-hole golf courses, tennis courts, 25 (yes, 25!) pools, formal gardens, and a date grove. The spacious and elegant rooms are located in adobe buildings. Expensive. 49-499 Eisenhower Drive, La Quinta, CA 92253. 619/564-4111; and 800/472-4316 in California, 800/854-1271 elsewhere in the United States.

✪ *Ritz-Carlton Rancho Mirage.* This elegant hotel has one attraction the other resorts in the desert cannot match. The hill behind the hotel is a sanctuary for bighorn sheep, and several times a day the magnificent animals wander onto the back lawn near the pool to munch on the plants. The animals are wild and they should be given some space. Otherwise, this is another elegant hotel, offering 240 luxury rooms, a heated pool, tennis courts, and a tennis center directed by U.S. Davis Cup Captain Tom Gorman. Expensive. 68-900 Frank Sinatra Drive, Rancho Mirage, CA 92270. 619/321-8282 and 800/241-3333 nationwide.

Rare Species Meets the Ritz

One of the delights of our stay at the Ritz-Carlton Rancho Mirage was the daily visit of the rare bighorn sheep. The sheep, about the size of a small pony, live on a rocky, seemingly barren hillside preserve immediately back of the elegant hotel.

Several times during our stay, groups of two or three sheep wandered onto the beautifully landscaped grounds, passing the pool as they headed to the flower garden near the terrace. The flowers are a favorite snack for the sheep, hotel officials told us, and cost the resort more than $1,000 a month in replantings.

Whatever the cost, the opportunity to see these magnificent wild animals up close was priceless. They seem to have no fear of man, but are wary about anyone who gets too close.

❂ *Stouffer Esmerelda.* There are 560 rooms at this sprawling sport-oriented resort. The rooms are large and nicely furnished. The real attraction is outdoors, where there are two 18-hole golf courses, tennis courts, a private beach, bicycles, two pools, lawn games, a health and fitness center, and health spa. Expensive. 44-400 Indian Wells Lane, Indian Wells, CA 92210. 619/773-4444.

❂ *Villa Royale.* The atmosphere is European in this cozy 34-room inn. The rooms are decorated with antiques and art from Europe and North Africa. Some rooms have fireplaces and jacuzzis. Moderate. 1620 Indian Trail, Palm Springs, CA 92264. 619/327-2314 and 800/245-2314 outside California nationwide.

Palm Springs: Fine Dining

❂ *Cactus Corral.* The specialty is barbecue but the real hot stuff is on the dance floor, where the local cowboys and cowgirls strut their stuff to a live country and western band. Moderate. 67-501 East Palm Canyon Drive, Cathedral City. 619/321-8558.

❂ *Cafe Cabo.* This new, chic Mexican restaurant is beautifully decorated and serves excellent food, cooked in an open kitchen, from all regions of that neighbor to the south. The appetizers are wonderful, but so large they can spoil your appetite for the main courses. Moderate. 125 East Tahquitz Canyon Way. 619/325-5270.

❂ *Las Casuelas Terraza.* This charming restaurant carries the Mexican decor a bit too far, but the authentic Mexican dishes will make you ignore the peasant costumes and mariachi band. Moderate. 222 South Palm Canyon Drive. 619/325-2794.

❂ *Cedar Creek Inn.* Beautiful gardenlike setting and a continental menu makes this a popular place with old hands of the desert spas. Moderate. 1555 South Palm Canyon Drive. 619/325-7300.

❂ *Cunard's.* This elegant villa serves up a menu of classic French and Italian dishes. Everything is excellent. Expensive. 73-045 Calle Cadiz, La Quinta. 619/564-4443.

❂ *Eleveen's.* Traditional French cuisine, with an emphasis on seafood dishes. Expensive. 664 North Palm Canyon Drive. 619/325-4766.

❂ *Mama Gina's.* The best Italian food (with the flavor of Tuscany) in the desert. Enough said. Expensive. 73-705 El Paseo, Palm Desert. 619/568-9898.

❂ *Melvyn's.* Popular with the wealthy set, this elegant European-style restaurant serves excellent continental cuisine. Expensive. 200 West Ramon Road. 619/325-2323.

❂ *Mille Fleurs.* Excellent continental dishes, particularly the seafood. Expensive. 73-101 Highway 111, Palm Desert. 619/773-3337.

❂ *El Mirasol.* Great Mexican food. Moderate. 140 East Palm Canyon Drive. 619/323-0721.

❂ *The Otani.* Fantastic Japanese cuisine in a beautiful garden with bamboo trees, a waterfall, and a brook. Expensive. 266 Avenida Caballeros. 619/327-6700.

❂ *Ritz-Carlton.* Excellent dining, with The Dining Room servicing classic French cuisine and the Cafe offering Californian cuisine and grilled entrees. The Cafe's Sunday brunch and Friday night seafood buffet are big hits. Call early for reservations. Both rooms are expensive. 68-900 Frank Sinatra Drive, Rancho Mirage. 619/ 321-8282.

❂ *Sorrento's.* Great seafood and lobster, but don't overlook the steak and veal osso buco genovese. Expensive. 1032 North Canyon Drive. 619/325-2944.

❂ *Le Vallauris.* Classic French cuisine served in an elegant restaurant that once was a private club. Expensive. 385 West Tahquitz-McCallum Way. 619/325-5059.

❂ *Vicki's of Sante Fe.* Lively atmosphere with dancing. Excellent American menu. Expensive. 45-100 Club Drive, Indian Wells. 619/345-9770.

The Mojave Desert and Death Valley: Romantic Lodging and Fine Dining

Lodging in this area is limited.

✪ *Furnace Creek Inn.* Located on Highway 190 just outside the park; it's a true oasis, offering 67 rooms in a sprawling stone building. The facilities include a dining room, tennis, golf, stables, and a heated pool. Expensive. Highway 190, P.O. Box 1, Death Valley, CA 92328. 619/786-2345.

For fine dining, try the inn's dining room, which serves an expensive continental menu.

Chapter Five

Murder, Music, Magic, and More

We weren't expecting trouble that weekend in the mountains. No, we just wanted to get away from the hassles of the city. Little did we know what we were getting into. Before the weekend was over, shots had been fired, bodies had been found, and the guilty parties unmasked.

Not, however, because of any crafty sleuthing we did.

Murder mystery weekends are popular and fun-filled diversions, offering a getaway with a purpose. In this case it was to catch a killer. We and the other guests taking part in the weekend sorted through the clues, gathering with the actors who staged the mystery twice a day for new clues and more action. It was great fun, a weekend that was a change from our usual escapes into art, antiques, and beautiful scenery.

If mysteries are not your mania, there are other weekends with a purpose available for couples seeking a different getaway. You can take part in one of the finest wine tastings on the West Coast, ride the range with real cowboys, pamper your body at an exclusive and luxurious spa, spend the night in a sheik's tent (or another room whose decor matches your secret fantasy), or even play a role in a musical or melodrama.

This chapter provides a compilation of some interesting getaways. Many book up early, so always make your reservations as far ahead as possible.

✪ MURDER, ANYONE?

✪ *An Elegant Victorian Mansion.* This 1888 Eastlake Victorian is the perfect setting for a murder. So perfect, in fact, that it happens once a month. Guests play parts in both the crime and the investigation. In addition, the inn has two antique cars—a 1928 Ford convertible and a 1930 Ford with a rumble seat—that guests can ride in. The inn has four guest rooms, filled with period antiques. There is an additional charge for the murder mystery. Rooms range from $75 to $100 a night. 1406 C Street, Eureka, CA 95501. 707/444-3144.

The locations of murder mystery weekends often change, so the best way to find out where the next killing is to take place is by calling the masterminds of crime, Murder Mystery Weekend and Dial M Murder Mystery. These killers-for-hire arrange deaths in hotels, on trains, and in elegant country inns. Call Murder Mystery Weekend at 818/785-7700, Dial M Murder Mystery at 818/953-4256. Go armed only with questions.

✪ WINE AND ROMANCE

✪ *Ye Olde Shelford House.* In the summer, this 1885 Victorian inn offers a leisurely tour of nearby wineries in a turn-of-the-century fringed surrey (used in the movie *Paint Your Wagon*). The

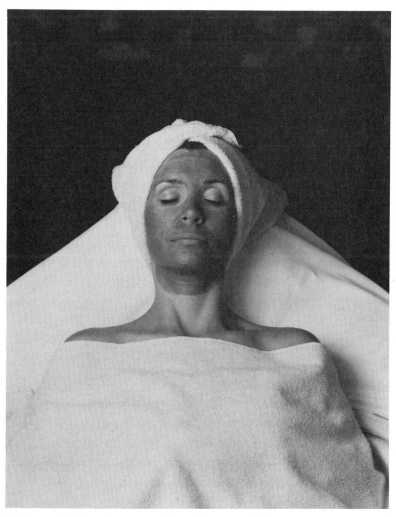

✪ The spa life: luxurious pampering and an escape from the real world. (Courtesy of the La Costa Resort and Spa)

ride costs $55 a couple and includes a picnic lunch and wine. The inn also offers a tour of five area wineries in an antique Model A Ford, followed by a picnic lunch at Lake Sonoma. That tour costs $60 a couple, including the picnic and wine. The inn is delightful, facing vineyards and offering six guest rooms filled with family heirlooms. The charges for the tasting tours are in addition to regular room rates, which range between $75 and $125. 29955 River Road, Cloverdale, CA 95425. 707/894-5956.

✪ *Ritz-Carlton Laguna Niguel.* This lavish resort, considered by many travel publications to be among the top five resort hotels in the nation, holds a World of Wines Festival every November. The festival is a weekend event, beginning with wine tastings at a buffet reception Friday evening and continuing on Saturday and Sunday with more tastings, seminars, receptions, and feasts. The sumptuous festival concludes with a black-tie gala, more wines, and wine talk. The rates range from $175 to $275 per night for the room plus a registration fee. The fee can be as low as about $150 per person for just the black-tie gala or as high as about $450 per person for all the events. 33533 Ritz-Carlton Drive, Laguna Niguel, CA 92677. 714/240-2000.

✪ PAMPER YOURSELF—SPAS AND RESORTS

✪ *Cal-A-Vie.* This exclusive mountaintop resort is known for its privacy and its ultrapampering program of massages, beauty treatments, and water therapies aimed at soothing your body and uplifting your soul. No more than 24 guests are housed in luxurious mountaintop villas during their weeklong stays. The pampering program features thalassotherapy, aromatherapy, and hydrotherapy to purify the body and rid it of wastes and toxins. The program also uses physical fitness tests, exercise, and diet programs. Facilities include a pool, whirlpool, sauna, exercise equipment, a tennis court, and an 18-hole golf course adjacent to the spa. The cost is $3,000 per person for a week. 2249 Somerset Road, Vista, CA 92084. 619/945-2055.

✪ *Claremont Spa.* Located in the Claremont Resort and Tennis Club, this fitness spa offers half-, one-day, and weekend programs and fitness evaluations. Facilities include the hotel's pool and tennis courts, a lap pool, exercise equipment, and an aerobics room. The cost begins at about $100 per person for the half-day and rises from there. P.O. Box 23363, Ashby and Domingo avenues, Oakland, CA 94623. 415/843-3000, ext. 200.

✪ *La Costa Hotel and Spa.* This is a big, beautiful resort, no doubt about it. Five swimming pools, 25 tennis courts, a theater, 2 golf courses, 510 rooms, and 1,000 acres of meticulously landscaped grounds. Spa guests are usually assigned rooms near the spa that are even larger than the spacious rooms found elsewhere in the resort. Guests can choose from massage therapists, exercise instructors, and programs on weight, diet, fitness, smoking, alcohol abuse, and stress management. Spa cuisine is offered, of course. Just stay away from the seven fine restaurants in the hotel, if you want to keep the weight off. The cost is $3,000 for a single, $4,600 for a couple. Costa Del Mar Road, Carlsbad, CA 92009. 619/438-9111; and 800/542-6200 in California, 800/854-6564 elsewhere in the United States.

✪ *The Golden Door.* Exclusive, expensive, and perhaps the ultimate in spa experiences, this luxurious spa offers personalized exercise and diet programs for its 39 guests. The guests have their own fitness counselor, uniforms to wear (meant to remove any individualism and trappings of wealth), a private room (even during the nine weeks set aside each year for couples), daily reports on skin, calorie-controlled meals, and plenty of time for exercise, meditation, and other spa-type activities. The cost is $3,500 per person for a week. Box 1567, Escondido, CA 92025. 619/744-5777.

✪ *Marriott's Desert Springs Resort and Spa.* In the middle of the desert the last thing one would expect at a spa—actually, anywhere—is lots of water. Yet there it is, millions of gallons in lagoons and pools surrounding this 892-room luxury spa that offers weeklong programs for beauty, fitness, weight control, and pampering. Facilities include 5 pools, a sauna, steam room, 2 golf courses, exercise equipment, and 23 tennis courts. The cost is $2,400 per week per person, plus a 12 percent service fee. 74855 Country Club Drive, Palm Desert, CA 92260. 619/341-2211, ext. 6278 and 800/255-0848 nationwide.

✪ *Mondrian Hotel.* Weekend spa programs are the specialty of this 186-room West Hollywood hotel. The weekends offer aerobics, yoga, diet modification, and massage. The cost is about $175 per person, breakfast included. Facilities include a pool, sauna, steam room, and exercise equipment. 8440 Sunset Boulevard, West Hollywood, CA 90069. 213/650-8999 and 800/244-4443.

✪ *Murrieta Hot Springs Resort and Health Spa.* This is a holistic retreat, offering weeklong programs in stress management, relationships, and health. The focus is on improving the management of your life. Facilities include 3 hot mineral spring pools, saunas, 14 tennis courts, golf, and exercise equipment. The cost is about $900 per person for a week. 39405 Murrieta Hot Springs Road, Murrieta, CA 92362. 714/677-7451.

✪ *The Oaks at Ojai.* This exclusive resort offers weeklong fitness and weight-loss programs. The Oaks has 43 rooms and accepts a maximum of 70 guests. The programs include nutrition, behavior modification, and improving your self-image. Facilities include pool, sauna, tennis, and exercise equipment. A week costs $700 per person. 122 East Ojai Avenue, Ojai, CA 93023. 805/646-5573.

✪ *The Palms at Palm Springs.* This exclusive resort is similar to the Oaks at Ojai. That's because they share one owner, Sheila Cluff. There are 43 rooms and a maximum of 85 guests at the Palms. The emphasis, as it is at the Oaks, is on weight loss and fitness through behavior modification and nutrition. Facilities include a pool, sauna, eight tennis courts, and exercise equipment. A week costs about $900 per person. 572 North Indian Avenue, Palm Springs, CA 92262. 619/325-1111.

❂ *Pritikin Longevity Center.* The spa claims their program is "an education in a new way of life." Yes, but it seems the classes are built around changing diet and exercise, particularly walking. The programs—either 13- or 26-day plans—are active and very scheduled. The Center has hotel rooms for 150 guests, pool, exercise equipment, and the beach. The cost ranges from $4,200 for 13 days ($5,500 for a couple) to $7,200 for 26 days ($9,600 for two). 1910 Ocean Front Walk, Santa Monica, CA 90405. 800/421-0981 in California, 800/421-9911 elsewhere in the United States.

❂ *Sonoma Mission Inn and Spa.* This pampering resort is in the middle of wine country. There are 170 rooms in the inn, but spa guests are limited to no more than 15. The programs include beauty treatments, massage, stretch and relax programs, yoga, and aerobics. The five-day programs cost $1,350 per person. Facilities include two pools, sauna, two tennis courts, and exercise equipment. 18140 Sonoma Highway, Boyes Hot Springs, CA 95416. 707/938-9000; and 800/862-4945 in California, 800/ 358-9022 elsewhere in the United States.

❂ *Spa Hotel & Mineral Springs.* Once a pampering resort, this spa is now emphasizing fitness. The hotel has 230 rooms, but the spa admits only 20 guests at a time. Programs last a week and include massage, mineral baths, hydrotherapy, walking, aerobics, lectures, and conditioning. Facilities include three pools (two fed by the hot springs), three tennis courts, and exercise equipment. The week costs about $750 per person. 100 North Indian Avenue, Palm Springs, CA 92262. 619/325-1461; and 800/472-4371 in California, and 800/854-1279 elsewhere in the United States.

❂ AN ARTS IMMERSION

❂ *Idyllwild School of Music and the Arts.* The location is striking: 205 acres in the San Jacinto Mountains between Los Angeles and the desert valleys. And the resort offers even more excitement: workshops in visual and applied arts, dance, theater, music, and Native American arts. The latter include the Mother Earth Father Sky classes on Hopi weaving, Acoma potterymaking, Cahuilla basketry, and mask-carving, sculpture, jewelry making and other Native American arts. More traditional classes include photography, painting, drawing, collage, writing, poetry, and sculpture. Housing is in motel-like units (tent sites are available for true nature lovers). Weekly rates start at about $300 per person, and include all meals. Write for a catalog of courses. P.O. Box 38, Idyllwild, CA 92349. 714/659-2171 and 213/622-0355.

❂ ESCAPES INTO FANTASIES

❂ *Archbishops Mansion.* The 15 guest rooms in this beautifully restored 1904 belle epoque inn furnished are named after nineteenth-century romantic operas and decorated in the theme. The opera connection, done lightly but nicely in the room decor, is because the San Francisco Opera is just 10 blocks away. Most of the rooms have fireplaces and great views of the city. Room rates are $100 to $285. 1000 Fulton Street, San Francisco, CA 94117. 415/563-7872 and 800/543-5820 nationwide.

❂ *Madonna Inn.* This castle comes complete with winding staircases, turrets, and 109 rooms—each with what one would call "individual decor." The rooms are fantasies, and are decorated in different themes. The Love Nest, for example, is a pink dream (or nightmare), the Cave Man has a leopard-skin bedspread and a waterfall shower, while the Safari Room has a big-game-hunter theme. You get the picture. It's, well, unusual. Room rates start at about $100 and rise sharply for the more popular rooms. 100 Madonna Road, San Luis Obispo, CA 93401. 805/543-3000.

❂ *Union Hotel.* The six fantasy rooms this hotel offers are located in a nearby Victorian mansion. The rooms are a testament to the spirit and creativity that makes America great. More than 200 artists, sculptors, and craftspeople have turned this mansion into rooms with such themes as a Sheik's Tent (harem bed, great view of an oasis), Fall of the Roman Empire (sleep in a chariot while Rome burns over the marble bath), Gypsy Caravan (hand-carved wagon bed), 1956 Drive-In (sleep in a 1956 Caddy convertible surrounded by neon lights while the movie *Rebel Without a Cause* plays), a Captain's Cabin (a mahogany pirate ship where you sleep in a bunk bed), and Paris of the 1800s (Lautrec's loft). It certainly is unique. Rooms start at $200 a night and include champagne. 362 Bell Street, Los Alamos, CA 93440. 805/344-2744.

❂ HOME ON THE RANGE

❂ *Circle Bar B Guest Ranch.* This 1,000-acre ranch in the Santa Ynez Mountains offers something for everyone. You can ride the ranch horses on half-day tours and join a square dance or take a role in a musical, comedy, or melodrama presented on weekday evenings. Guests stay in six cabins or the five rooms in the ranch house. Facilities include a pool. Daily rates start at about $130 per person for the ranch house, higher for the cabins. Rates include all meals, but not horses or theater. 1800 Refugio Road, Goleta, CA 93117. 805/968-1113.

❂ *M Bar J Guest Ranch.* Bordered by the Sequoia National Park, guests at this old family ranch in the Sierra foothills can ride through the wildflowers in the park, hike in the hills, or just relax around the pool. You can go cross-country skiing in the park through April. Guests stay in eight cabins and two mobile homes (choose the cabins). Activities include square dancing, trail parties, and cookouts. Weekly rates range from about $550 per person and up, all meals and horses included. The ranch is open mid-March through September. Box 67G, Badger, CA 93603. 209/337-2513.

✪ *Montecito-Sequoia Lodge.* Located at 7,500 feet between the scenic Sequoia and Kings Canyon national parks, this year-round ranch offers horseback riding, canoeing, fishing in mountain streams, and visiting artists who give instruction in painting. There are 35 nice lodge rooms with private baths and 23 rustic cabins with 3 bathhouses. Daily rates start at about $85 per person and include all meals. Rates are lower in the winter. A special bargain is the bed-and-breakfast rate for two (about $75). 1485-RV Redwood, Los Altos, CA 94022. 415/967-8612; and 800/227-9900 in California, 800/451-1505 elsewhere in the United States.

✪ *San Ysidro Ranch.* Popular with Hollywood names, this secluded, 540-acre luxury ranch has 43 rooms set in quaint cottages spread around 14 acres of gardens and orange trees. The rooms are luxurious and the style is very casual, except at dinner, when things become formal. Amenities include a pool, tennis courts, horseback riding, and golf nearby. Room rates start at $165 per day and rise rapidly to more than $400 for the suites with private hot tubs. Meals and horses are not included. 900 San Ysidro Lane, Montecito, CA 93108. 805/969-5046.

✪ *Spanish Springs Ranch.* This is a real spread: 50,000 acres, with pastures, mountains, and lakes. You can stay in a new cabin and eat western-style meals at the lodge or stay in the more rustic old homesteads out on the range. There you can ride out with the cowboys when they herd the cattle. The ranch is home to buffalo, antelope, and wild horses. Facilities include an indoor pool, tennis, and volleyball. Riding lessons, guided trail rides, moonlight hayrides, and campfire barbecues and singalongs are also offered. In the winter, guests can go cross-country skiing over the vast ranch or take a sleigh ride. It's all so wonderful! Weekly rates are about $750 per person and include all meals. Daily rates available on request. The ranch is near Ravendale, about 2 hours north of Reno. 1102 Second Street, San Rafael, CA 94901. 415/485-5556; and 800/272-8282 in California, 800/228-0279 elsewhere in the United States.

✪ SPECIALTY RESORTS

This Room Is Rocking

✪ *Bed and Breakfast San Francisco.* Stay aboard a banker's 47-foot luxury yacht with the best view of the skyline. You sleep in a queen-size bed and have a television and all other modern conveniences. The cost is $200 a night. P.O. Box 349, San Francisco, CA 94101. 415/931-3083.

4 Rm, Bay Vu

✪ *East Brother Light Station.* This Victorian lighthouse, located on an island in San Francisco Bay, may offer the ultimate in rooms with a view. There are four guest rooms—two in the lighthouse, two in an adjacent guest house. The rooms are small but adequately furnished. Guests are taken to the island by boat from the San Pablo Yacht Harbor. The rooms start at more than $200. 117 Park Place, Point Richmond, CA 94801. 415/233-2385 and 415/ 990-5834.

In Days of Yore

✪ *Ahwahnee Hotel.* Queen Elizabeth stayed here. Ditto the Shah, Charlie Chaplin, a few kings and queens, and Emperor

Selassie. But even they would have had to make reservations far in advance to get a room at this grand, wood-and-stone mountain lodge in Yosemite for the annual Bracebridge Renaissance Christmas Feast and musical celebration. More than 10,000 try to take part, but only the fortunate few make it. There are 123 rooms in the main hotel and the cottages. Rates start at $175. Yosemite Park & Curry Company, Central Reservations, 5410 East Home, Fresno, CA 93727. 209/252-4848.

What's Playing Tonight?

✪ *Benbow Inn.* If you ever wanted to catch up on all those old movies you missed, come to this inn, where more than 250 classics of cinema are available for guests on request. The movies are shown in a small theater. The elegant Tudor inn has been visited by Eleanor Roosevelt, Charles Laughton, and other celebrities seeking the serenity and beauty of the Redwood Empire. The 55 rooms are comfortable, and decorated with art, antiques, and collectibles. The inn also has a Halloween Masquerade Ball. The inn is on the Eel River and is near the Avenue of the Giants. Rates start at about $100 and rise, according to the room and season. 445 Lake Benbow Drive, Garberville, CA 95440. 707/923-2124.

Lights! Cameras! Action!

✪ *Circle Bar B Guest Ranch.* Guests at this 1,000-acre ranch in the Santa Ynez Mountains not only can ride the range, but they take part in the musicals, comedies, or melodramas presented on weekday evenings. If you can still move after a day in the saddle, try kicking up your heels at a square dance. Daily rates start at about $130, and include all meals, but not horses or theater. 1800 Refugio Road, Goleta, CA 93117. 805/968-1113.

Chapter Six

Tales of Three Cities

San Francisco sees itself as a genteel city, a center of culture where history and family are important. The fact that the city overlooks a gorgeous bay and a picturesque bridge is only proper.

Los Angeles has the self-made image as the trend arbiter for the world, the place where the "ins"—foods, activities, fads, restaurants, movie stars, night clubs, and fashion—are transitory and can become "outs" almost overnight. Los Angeles is often just a beautiful illusion, which is appropriate for a place that's synonymous with Hollywood.

San Diego is the underrated city, one often derided by its two cosmopolitan and haughty sister cities to the north as a town built around a Navy base. Yet it is in San Diego that the Californian lifestyle celebrating the outdoors and recreation can be combined with culture.

Three cities, three lifestyles, and three wonderful getaways.

You can visit them for a weekend or a lifetime, but don't miss these delightful places.

✪ LOS ANGELES

The numbers on Los Angeles give you a feel for the city: 4,083 square miles, more than 9 million residents, and more cars than in all of New York State. But the numbers don't tell you Los Angeles has beaches as well as mountains, endless tracts of look-alike houses as well as magnificent mansions, and a world of other attractions, some real, some illusions.

There is so much to see. Hollywood, theaters, museums, historic pueblos, beautiful beaches, ethnic neighborhoods, picturesque suburbs, the homes of the stars, television studios, and some of the ritziest shops ever. Getting around by car is usually easy. Parking is plentiful and traffic isn't a horror if you avoid the freeways and the daily rush hours.

The places we found interesting and romantic are around the west side, in the city center, and along the Pacific coast. A few diversions—the studios, Disneyland, and the scenic canyon roads—take you further afield. To help you share these delights, we divided Los Angeles into these suggested tours: Downtown, Hollywood, the Westside, the Pacific Coast, and other diversions.

When you visit, there is another drive to take, a mountaintop road that offers some of the most stunning views of the city and the San Fernando Valley. The road is Mulholland Drive, and you can get on this 55-mile highway on the top of the Santa Monica Mountains by taking Laurel Canyon, Coldwater Canyon, Benedict Canyon, or Beverly Glen roads from Sunset Boulevard. Driving this mountaintop highway is often a slow process, for the road twists and each turn offers a new breathtaking view of the city and valley.

If the night is clear, drive to the parking turnoff on Mulholland just east of Benedict Canyon Road. At night, the lights of the city and valley fill the world below. The sight is incredible.

Downtown

Start your tour where it all began, at El Pueblo de Los Angeles Historic Monument at 845 North Alameda Street. The first settlement was built here in 1781. The park comprises 44 acres and contains 27 historic buildings around a plaza and Olvera Street. The Avila Adobe on Olvera Street was built in 1818 and is the oldest building in town.

The park is like a Mexican marketplace, complete with cobblestone streets, entertainment, food, and other attractions. On weekends, the street and park are filled with folk dancers and musicians. The kiosko, the nineteenth-century bandstand, is the site of concerts of Mexican and Spanish music. The puestos—tiny stands where vendors sell Mexican food—are great places to get an interesting snack.

From this point you can walk north to two major ethnic neighborhoods: Chinatown north of Sunset Boulevard between Hill Street and North Broadway and Little Tokyo south of the Hollywood Freeway around Los Angeles and Second streets. Both neighborhoods are colorful, with shops selling exotic produce, a few fine restaurants, and scads of stores selling a wide variety of merchandise.

Three blocks east of Little Tokyo, at Third and Broadway, is the Central Market, a bazaar of vegetables, meats, and other foodstuffs. It's a good place to browse or to pick up a quick snack from the Mexican vendors in the market.

Both Chinatown and Little Tokyo are crowded, fascinating neighborhoods, full of colorful sights, wonderful smells, and exotic festivals. Check the Los Angeles tourism office for the current festival schedule.

Farther east at First Street and Grand Avenue is the Music Center, the cultural mecca of the city with three theaters. The largest theater is the 2,000-seat Ahmanson Theater; it's the showcase for plays. The Dorothy Chandler Pavilion is where the Los Angeles Philharmonic, Civil Light Opera, and other classical music and dance troupes perform. The third theater is the Mark Taper Forum, a 742-seat playhouse featuring plays by new artists. Box offices for all three are located at the Music Center at 135 North Grand Avenue.

Two blocks south of the theater complex, at 250 South Grand Avenue, is the Museum of Contemporary Art, with works by Franz Kline, Mark Rothko, Jackson Pollock, and other artists.

Hollywood

The sign—Hollywood, in white letters 45 feet high and stretching 450 feet long—is at the top of Beachwood Canyon, about a mile east of the fabled intersection of Hollywood and Vine. The sign was erected in 1923 to promote a real estate development named Hollywoodland. After World War II, the "land" part was removed, creating the world-famous landmark that is visible for miles.

The sign appears unchanged by time. You can't say that about Hollywood and Vine. Once a legendary intersection where starlets were found, Hollywood and Vine is now a bit seedy. Some landmarks remain, unchanged by the years. The Capitol Records building, at 1756 North Vine, still looks like a stack of 45s (although the CD generation may not know what those are). The Palace, called the Hollywood Playhouse (1735 North Vine) when it opened in 1927, now shakes to rock concerts.

A short walk west of Hollywood and Vine is the Hollywood

✪ The famous foot- and handprints of the stars at Mann's Chinese Theatre in Hollywood. (Courtesy of the Los Angeles Convention & Visitors Bureau)

Walk of Fame, on Hollywood Boulevard between Gower and Sycamore streets (see box). Farther west at 6608 on the boulevard is the infamous Frederick's of Hollywood, the original designer of the less-is-more look, and Mann's Chinese Theatre, the gaudy pagoda once known as Grauman's Chinese Theatre. Mann's is known for its hand- and footprints of celebrities in its interior courtyard.

On these streets of dreams, the past is not only remembered, it's for sale. Book City Collectibles (6631 Hollywood Boulevard) offers a wide collection of autographs of such stars as Lucille Ball, Anthony Hopkins, Grace Kelly, and Leslie Howard as well as more than 70,000 photographs. The Hollywood Book and Poster Company (6349 Hollywood Boulevard) sells scripts, posters, and other tinseltown memorabilia. Some real old items, including stills of Laurel and Hardy collected by producer Hal Roach, are on sale at The Last Moving Picture Show (6307 Hollywood Boulevard).

North of the boulevard, on Highland Avenue, is the famous Hollywood Bowl, still a popular place for concerts. In the parking lot is the Lasky–de Mille Barn, where Cecil B. de Mille produced his first movie, *The Squaw Man*, in 1913. In 1927, the barn became the headquarters of Paramount Pictures. The barn was moved to its present site and turned into the Hollywood Studio Museum, exhibiting cameras, props, costumes, and other memorabilia from Hollywood's early days.

Another Hollywood attraction is a monument to a giant in architecture. In Barnsdall Park (4800 Hollywood Boulevard) is the Hollyhock House, the first house ever designed by the famous architect Frank Lloyd Wright. The house was built in 1921 for an heiress and is done in pre-Columbian style. It has been restored and furnished with furniture designed by Wright.

Westside

The names are famous throughout the world: Bel Air, Beverly Hills, Rodeo Drive, Wilshire Boulevard, Benedict Canyon, and Sunset Boulevard.

This is the playground of the rich and famous. Here the attractions are exclusive shops and restaurants, trendy nightclubs, magnificent hotels, and mansions that expand the meaning of luxurious. Not everyone on these streets is rich or famous; people watching is a popular pastime, and far easier on your credit rating.

The main thoroughfare on the Westside is Wilshire Boulevard, which stretches 16 miles from the center of the city to the coast. A drive along Wilshire is like a cross-section of L.A. On its eastern end, Wilshire starts in the Hispanic barrios in the center of the city

Where the Stars Are

You don't need a map to find the stars. Some have their favorite hangouts. Here is a quick primer to star gazing:

The hot spot for stars from all walks of life is Spago (1114 Horn Avenue, West Hollywood). For studio heads and agents and, occasionally, Kevin Costner, visit Morton's (8800 Melrose Avenue, West Hollywood). Another West Hollywood spot (though not as hot as it once was) is Chasen's (9039 Beverly Boulevard). It remains popular with Sinatra, James Stewart, Ron and Nancy Reagan, and Elizabeth Taylor (she loves the chili).

The coast has star sightings. Patrick's Roadhouse (106 Entrada Drive), a bright green saloon just off the Pacific Coast Highway in Santa Monica, is a hangout for Arnold and Maria Schwarzenegger. The couple usually dines at one of the two tables up the steps from the counter. The muscleman and pal Clint Eastwood (can you imagine telling them the kitchen is out of an entree?) have been sighted at Ivy at the Shore (1541 Ocean Avenue, Santa Monica).

Ivy (113 North Robertson Boulevard), the Ivy at the Shore's sister restaurant, is favored by rocker George Michael, "home-movie star" Rob Lowe, and "shredder of the year" Fawn Hall.

and moves west through aging Victorian neighborhoods until it comes to La Brea Avenue and the art deco buildings of the stretch called the Miracle Mile when it was developed in the 1930s. The Bullock's Wilshire (3050 Wilshire), the green terra-cotta of the Wiltern Theatre (3790 Wilshire), and the Darkroom (5370 Wilshire) are outstanding examples of this architectural style.

Farther west is Hancock Park, home to the George C. Page Museum of La Brea Discoveries, which has more than a million fossils from the Ice Age. The museum is next to the La Brea Tar Pits (*brea* means "tar" in Spanish, so the name is a bit redundant), whose sticky ooze captured the largest known collection of Ice Age fossils ever found.

In the next block is the Los Angeles County Museum of Art, a multibuilding complex that displays works by Picasso, Rembrandt, Homer, and La Tour as well as works from the Orient. The Ahmanson Gallery holds works by the European masters and a broad collection of art from India, Tibet, and Nepal. The Robert O. Anderson Building showcases twentieth-century art, traveling exhibitions, and Japanese art, including a prize collection of 300 Japanese scroll paintings. The Leo S. Bing Center has museum shops, theater, library, and an indoor/outdoor cafe.

Across from the museum is the Craft and Folk Art Museum (5814 Wilshire), which displays superb crafts and folk art from around the world.

After these museums, you may continue west to the Regent Beverly Wilshire Hotel, the luxury hotel popular with stars and visiting personages but made even more famous as the setting for the recent hit movie *Pretty Woman.*

The hotel is a great place to stroll through (the lobby looks a lot smaller than it did in the movie) or a stop for a drink or lunch. You may need to regain your strength, for right outside the doors is the shopping district even more famous than the hotel. The triangle bordered by Wilshire, Santa Monica Boulevard, and Rexford Drive is called the Golden Triangle by locals, but the world knows it by one name: Rodeo Drive.

Rodeo Drive is the home to some of the most exclusive, expensive, and exotic shops in the world. Chanel (301 North Rodeo Drive), Tiffany & Co. (210 North Rodeo Drive), Gianni Versace (437 North Rodeo Drive), and Bardelli (335 North Rodeo Drive) offer items to bust a budget, while Fred Hayman (273 North Rodeo Drive) not only sells stylish fashions for men and women but invites its customers to relax at the magnificent oak bar separating the two sections of the store. Even more sumptuous is Bijan (420

Santa Catalina Island

Picture an island 22 miles offshore from one of the world's biggest cities. Then picture this unspoiled wilderness island without the traffic, without the development, without any of the stressful aspects of Southern California. If you can picture that, you have a clear image of what Santa Catalina is like.

William Wrigley of chewing-gum fame bought the island and kept it closed to outsiders until 1929 when he built the elegant Casino—a dance hall, not a gambling emporium. The Casino became nationally famous through radio broadcasts of its dances that featured such bands as Benny Goodman and Kay Kyser.

The Casino is in Avalon, the only city on the almost unspoiled 21-mile-long island. You can rent a bike or golf cart from vendors in Avalon. The sights include the museum, movie house, art gallery in the Casino, and the Wrigley Memorial and Botanical Gardens, 2 miles south of town.

If you want to make a weekend of your visit, the Zane Grey Pueblo Hotel (it really was the author's home; 213/510-0966) and the Victorian-style Hotel Catalina (213/510-0027) offer nice rooms at moderate rates. For sheer elegance, you can't beat the Inn at Mt. Ada, the former Wrigley Mansion that has six luxurious rooms, stunning views, and wonderful gardens. Expensive, but worth it. Call 213/510-2030.

You can visit Avalon and the island by taking the Catalina Express from San Pedro or Long Beach. Call 213/519-1212. Catalina Passenger Service runs ferries from the Balboa Pavilion at Newport Beach. Call 714/673-5245. The fare is between $25 and $30, roundtrip.

North Rodeo Drive), where you cannot shop on an impulse. At Bijan, you will need an appointment (call 213/273-6544).

The exclusive shops extend to the streets east and west of Rodeo Drive. These shops are no less elegant or exotic. One small

Walks of the Stars

Even the first-time visitor to California knows about the Hollywood Walk of Fame where stars are enshrined in pink stars with a brass nameplate and Mann's (call it Grauman's Chinese and you'll reveal your age) Chinese Theatre's autographed hand- and footprints in the concrete of the courtyard.

But even the most savvy tinseltown tourist may miss those other Walks of Fame. These are the Walk of Western Stars, the Rock Walk, the Avenue of Athletes, and the Orange County Walk of Stars. Here is a rundown on all six attractions:

Hollywood Walk of Fame. *There are almost 2,000 names in this star-studded sidewalk. It begins at the northwest corner of Highland Avenue and Hollywood Boulevard and continues along the boulevard and Vine Street. The stars pay for the honor (it costs a bit under $4,000), and many of the names are from Hollywood's first years and are not household names. Marilyn Monroe's star is at 6774 Hollywood Boulevard (a block from the original Frederick's of Hollywood at 6608 Hollywood Boulevard), John Wayne at 1541 Vine Street, and Clark Gable at 1608 Vine Street.*

Mann's Chinese Theatre. *Located at 6925 Hollywood Boulevard. The theater, a combination of Chinese pagodas and modern kitsch, is an attraction by itself. To see the hand- and footprints of the stars, you'll have to buy a movie ticket. 213/464-8111.*

Walk of Western Stars. *Roy Rogers, Tom Mix, John Wayne, Tex Ritter, and 28 other western stars are enshrined at this walk along San Fernando Road at Fifth Street in Newhall, in the valley north of Los Angeles. The cowpokes' names are in silver stars in a setting of bronze and terrazzo.*

The Rock Walk. *Stevie Wonder, B. B. King, Bo Diddley, and about three dozen other rock 'n' roll greats are enshrined in this walk in front of the Guitar Center (7425 Sunset Boulevard).*

Avenue of Athletes. *The markers honoring more than 30 local jocks such as Kareem Abdul-Jabbar, Billie Jean King,*

Jackie Robinson, and Tommy Lasorda are tiny brass plates on Sunset Boulevard between Echo Park Avenue and Alvarado Street.

The Orange County Walk of Stars. Donny Osmond (!), Joey Bishop (!!). It's hard to understand why, but these two are honored along with other Orange County celebs in the walk in front of the Anaheim Hilton and Towers at 777 Convention Way across from Disneyland.

---

store, the Caviarteria at 247 North Beverly Drive, sells only the finest caviar.

Another shopping mecca is along Melrose Avenue just west of Beverly Hills. On the avenue, Melrose Place, and the adjacent blocks of Robertson and La Cienega are antique and art galleries and fine clothing shops. Take time to visit Lion et La Licorne (8445 Melrose Avenue), Panache (8445 Melrose Avenue), Licorne (8432 Melrose Place), Rose Tarlow Antiques (8454 Melrose Place), Phyllis Lapham's Antiques (8422 Melrose Place), La Maison Francaise Antiques (don't be put off by the small entrance; 8420 Melrose Place), and Paul Ferrante (8464 Melrose Place).

Antique shops aren't the only attractions. Betsey Johnson (7311 Melrose Avenue) offers clothing that can best be described as dressing in less (but *not* for less). Star Rags (7303 Melrose Avenue) sells pieces of clothing worn by Madonna, Cher, Rod Stewart, and other stars, while Bleeker Bob's (7663 Melrose) sells records from the 1960s.

The proliferation of these elegant boutiques and galleries can be easily explained: the homes of some of the wealthiest people in the world are just a short drive away. Beverly Hills, long associated with movie stars and wealth, is a separate city of about 34,000 residents living in a little under 6 square miles. It's a beautiful city, one best toured by car.

The main roads are Rodeo and Canyon drives north of Wilshire,

Sunset Boulevard, and the Benedict Canyon Drive. Driving them takes you past some magnificent homes, with the most lavish hiding behind walls of stone and shrubbery. Movie stars still live here, and you can buy a map to their homes from sidewalk vendors on Sunset Boulevard or in most stores and hotels. You won't see much, though, for wealth and celebrity brings walls, guards, and gates. A better way to see the sights of Beverly Hills and Hollywood would be to take the Hollywood Fantasy Tour, a guided 2- to 4-hour tour of more than 70 stars' homes, Rodeo Drive, Paramount Studios, and other attractions. Call 213/469-8184.

Another famous thoroughfare on the Westside is Sunset Boulevard. Like Wilshire, it begins downtown and heads west to the coast, intersecting with canyon roads and passing through Beverly Hills and Bel Air on its way to the sea.

For much of its 25-mile length, particularly in the downtown area, Sunset Boulevard is a busy commercial thoroughfare. Sunset Plaza, at La Cienega, offers boutiques and art galleries and some nice restaurants. Butterfield's Restaurant (8426 Sunset Boulevard) was once the home of Lionel Barrymore, and Greystone Mansion (905 Loma Vista Drive on the hill above the crossing of Sunset and Doheny Road) was built by oilman Edward Doheny in 1923, a few years before he got tarred by the Teapot Dome scandal. If the Tudor mansion looks familiar, perhaps it is because it was used as a setting in the film *The Witches of Eastwick*.

Sunset Boulevard continues west, passing through the haute mansions of Beverly Hills and Bel Air and the sprawling campus of UCLA before reaching the Pacific coast.

The Pacific Coast

Highway 1, better known as the Pacific Coast Highway, is the street of dreams along the coast of Los Angeles. On the north is Malibu, the trendy beach colony whose high-priced homes are hidden behind guardhouses and community gates. On the south is Marina del Rey, an upscale houses-and-highrises development built around marinas. In between these two golden retreats are beachfront parks, funky neighborhoods, great restaurants, and the finest museum in Los Angeles.

Begin a tour of the coast north of Malibu, where the Santa Monica Mountains drop abruptly to the sea. Leo Carillo State Beach, Zuma Beach County Park, and Point Dune Beach offer fine swimming, surfing, and people watching.

A nice serene retreat in this area is Malibu Creek State Park. Take N1 (the Malibu Canyon Road) into the 6,000-acre park and its Century Lake. The lake is rimmed by 300-year-old oaks and graced by mariposa lilies and other flowering plants and shrubs. The park was used as the setting for the TV series "M*A*S*H."

Return to the coast and drive south on Highway 1, passing by beach colonies, some modern hillside mansions, and the bright-green Patrick's Roadhouse (Arnold Schwarzenegger hangs out here) until you come to the turn inland for the J. Paul Getty Museum (17985 West Pacific Coast Highway).

The museum is a copy of the Villa Papyri at Herculaneum, destroyed in A.D. 79 by the eruption of Vesuvius. It was built in the mid-1970s at a cost of about $17 million to house the massive art and antiquities collection of Getty, a billionaire oilman and industrialist.

The museum is a peaceful oasis, cut off from the busy Highway 1 and the upscale houses on the hills above it. Stroll the grounds and you will see and hear songbirds, catch a glimpse of a flitting ruby-throated hummingbird, and just enjoy a moment of relaxation surrounded by a deep, rich green landscape.

The Getty collection is extensive and includes such major works as Vincent van Gogh's "Irises," paintings by Rembrandt, Rubens, Van Dyck, and Gainsborough, illuminated Renaissance manuscripts, decorative arts, fourth-century funery monuments, statues, and other pieces. Parking reservations are a must (you will be towed if you park in the neighborhood). On some summer evenings, concerts are held on the grounds. Call 213/458-2003 for parking and the concert schedule.

After this fabulous museum, continue driving south on Highway 1 through Malibu, where the coastal homes and restaurants are a bit commercial and tacky, and on to Santa Monica.

When you can, turn left onto Ocean Avenue and continue south on this higher road until you come to Palisades Park, a pleasant stretch of green overlooking the sea. In this park area, Santa Monica resembles Nice and its Promenade des Anglais.

At the south end of the park is the famous Santa Monica Pier, which has a colorful carousel (used in the movie *The Sting*), cafes, arcades, and a world of street characters.

After a spin on the carousel, consider driving south on Ocean Avenue to Pico Boulevard. Turn left and drive to Main Street, and then turn right again at 2437 Main Street and the Santa Monica Museum of Art, with works by performance and video artists. Two blocks further south at 2612 Main is the Santa Monica Heritage Museum, a restored Victorian mansion that is a museum to that era as well as an anchor to this reborn neighborhood of cafes, galleries, and eclectic shops.

Continue south on Main Street until you come to Venice Boulevard and turn right for a visit to one of L.A.'s funkiest towns. Venice was created in 1905 by a developer who wanted to create a replica of the more famous Italian city. He built 30 miles of canals, bridges, and an oceanfront park. Only 3 miles of canals still exist, and the neighborhood hasn't withstood the ravages of time as well as its Italian namesake.

Venice went through all the faddish movements of the postwar era: beat, Bohemia, and the psychedelic years of the 1960s. The middle class fled, street people moved in, and Venice deteriorated.

In recent years, Venice has been reawakened, if not reborn. First artists and then yuppies discovered the low housing prices. New shops opened, followed by innovative restaurants, which in turn brought more rehabs.

There are still some odd street characters to be found, and some streets are not as nice as the rehabbed areas. But Venice remains a funky and fascinating place. Venice Boulevard runs into the beachfront park, an area where the bodybuilders flex their pecs, rollerbladers whiz along the boardwalk, and vendors sell everything imaginable.

Venice's colorful atmosphere is a sharp contrast to its gold-card neighbors to the south. Marina del Rey, a modern complex of high-rise luxury condos, elegant waterfront homes and town-houses, restaurants, and pleasure boats, is the epitome of everything Southern California is known for: upscale housing, marinas stocked with luxury boats, fancy sports cars, and chic, tanned residents.

It's all very nice, and *so* California. It's just not as interesting as Venice.

Other Diversions

This is the capital of entertainment, and no visit to the City of Angels would be complete without a tour of the studios, a visit to Mickey's park, and a visit to a town that sees itself as a more refined city than its infamous and notorious neighbor.

For a behind-the-curtain look at television, you can attend a free taping of such shows as "Perfect Strangers," "Major Dad," and "Married with Children" (or their replacements, when ratings eventually fall). Tickets for the studios are available through Audiences Unlimited, whose main office is at Fox Television (5746 Sunset Boulevard; 818/506-0067). Warner Bros. Studios opens tapings of "Night Court," "Murphy Brown," and other shows (4000 Warner Boulevard, Burbank; 818/954-1744); CBS has "The Price is Right" and other game shows (7800 Beverly Boulevard; 213/852-2624); NBC has the "Tonight Show" (3000 West Alameda Avenue, Burbank; 818/840-3537); and Paramount opens "Arsenio Hall" and other shows (860 North Gower Avenue; 213/856-5575).

The best of the studio tours is found at Universal Studios in Universal City at the Hollywood Freeway and Lankershim Boulevard. Be certain to take the tram tour of such movie sets as *Back to the Future, Psycho,* and *The Burbs* as well as three-dimensional visits to stage sets with such special effects as King Kong, an earthquake, and an avalanche. Other attractions include restaurants, rides, entertainment, and countless souvenir shops. Call 818/508-9600.

The granddaddy (or grandmouse) of theme parks is Disneyland (1313 Harbor Boulevard in Anaheim, south of Los Angeles proper). It's as wonderful as ever, and is now expanding.

Finally, a visit to Los Angeles should include time for a tour of the San Gabriel Valley and Pasadena, the grand dame of Southern California.

This valley, one of three that make up the greater Los Angeles area, is lush. Pasadena, better known as the home of the Rose Bowl and Rose Parade, is an attractive community, with fine homes on nicely shaded streets.

The major attractions include the Norton Simon Museum at Orange Grove and Colorado boulevards, which features an excellent collection of Southeast Asian, Indian, and European masters.

After visiting the museum drive east on Colorado Boulevard for a half mile until you come to Old Town, a renovated area of shops, homes, and restaurants.

Other attractions in Pasadena include the Pacific Asia Museum (46 North Los Robles Drive), a garish palace with a superb collection of Asian and Polynesian arts and crafts.

In San Marino, just east of Pasadena, is the crown jewel of the valley: the Huntington Library, Art Gallery, and Botanical Gardens. The 200-acre estate (1151 Oxford Road) was once the home of railroad and electrical power baron Henry E. Huntington.

The mansion has 22 galleries of art and is widely acknowledged as the finest collection of eighteenth-century British art. The collection includes Gainsborough's original "Blue Boy" and the "Sarah Siddons as the Tragic Muse" by Reynolds.

The 130-acre garden has a cacti garden, a Japanese garden, and extensive displays of camellias, azaleas, roses, herbs, and jungle plants.

The library (the white classic structure next to the mansion) holds a half-million rare volumes and more than 5 million rare manuscripts, including a Gutenberg Bible, Shakespeare folios, and writings by George Washington.

✪ SAN DIEGO

The third city on the West Coast, San Diego, is many things. It's an old town, with a colonial heritage that dates back to 1542. In addition, it's a military town, one with big naval and air bases placed around the great, deep water bay. It's a sports town, with scores of golf courses and tennis courts, miles of jogging trails, parks for sailors, long beaches for swimmers and surfers, and inland mountains that challenge hikers and nature lovers. It's a town of clean air, pleasant ocean breezes, and an average temperature of 70 degrees. And it's a town of historic neighborhoods offering fascinating buildings, fine shops, and interesting restaurants.

The major attractions are widely dispersed in the city and county, so you will need a car. Traffic is usually light, parking is plentiful, and, in most cases, the roads are well marked. To help you enjoy this surprising interesting city, we have broken the attractions into On the Water, Downtown, and Sidetrips.

On the Water

San Diego's waterfront offers something for everyone. It has miles of wide beaches, tall cliffs abutting the churning seas, busy harborfronts with cruise ships and old sailing ships, water parks with a boatload of recreational activities, and coastal areas with fine shops and art galleries. The best way to get a bird's-eye view of the coast and harbor is by going to the oldest historic site in San Diego—Point Loma.

In 1542, Portuguese explorer Juan Rodriguez Cabrillo discovered a windswept promontory overlooking a majestic natural bay. Cabrillo called his discovery San Miguel. Sixty years later, Sebastian Vizcaino also discovered the great bay, but he named it San Diego. Despite its natural advantages as a harborage, the bay area wasn't settled until 1769 when the Spanish Father Junipero Serra, founder of the other great California missions, established Mission San Diego de Acala near the great bay.

The discovery by Cabrillo is remembered at that promontory, now called Point Loma. The peninsula curves around San Diego west of the airport, sheltering the city and the great bay. Walkways along the 400-foot-high cliffs offer great views of the sea, while other overlooks present stunning vistas of the bay, San Diego, and the mountains north and east of the city.

North of Point Loma is Sunset Cliffs, another ocean overlook. It's a popular place for watching the sun go down, but be careful walking along the edge. The caution signs are for real. Ocean erosion has made some areas of the cliffs unsafe.

South of Point Loma, across the narrow channel, is Coronado, an isthmus that is often mistaken for an island. Coronado, reached by ferry or bridge, is a low-key community with some fine Victorian homes, a naval air station and amphibious base; a grand old Victorian resort hotel, and some of the finest beaches in California. The popular swimming spots include the Coronado Beach, a wide stretch of sand with rest rooms, fire rings, athletic fields, and a backdrop of the famous red-and-white Victorian masterpiece called the Hotel del Coronado. The hotel is a popular tourist attraction, offering a beautiful carved, dark wood interior, fine shops, and a wide selection of restaurants.

If you prefer a quiet stretch of sand, head north or south of the hotel. The beaches are long, parking areas infrequent but available, and the crowds are basically nonexistent. These beaches are great for Frisbee, sunbathing, or jogging.

Coronado's offbeach attractions include a wide selection of shops and restaurants along Orange Avenue from the Hotel del Coronado east to the bay.

Back on the mainland, San Diego's other waterfront attractions are at the harbor and in a marine park north of the downtown. The Embarcadero along Harbor Drive just west of the downtown has several interesting attractions. At Ash Street and Harbor Drive is the Star of India, a restored windjammer built in 1863. It's part of the Maritime Museum, located in the Berkeley, a 93-year-old paddleboat by the B Street pier. The pier is the place to catch the ferry to Coronado.

A block inland of the pier, at Broadway and Kettner Boulevard, is the Santa Fe Depot, a marvelous old structure that has been restored and turned into a tourist information center and a depot for the tour buses for Mexico. Shops and restaurants are planned for the depot.

Continue south on Harbor Drive until it meets the water and turns, passing the Seaport Village, a 14-acre shopping and dining mall.

The other waterfront attraction in San Diego is Mission Bay Park, a 4,600-acre playland with 27 miles of beaches, water sports, and a marine park. Take Interstate 5 north to the East Misson Bay

✪ The magnificent Hotel del Coronado, a Victorian landmark on the beach in Coronado. (Courtesy of the Hotel del Coronado)

Drive exit. The Visitors Center (2688 East Mission Bay Drive) is an excellent source of information on park activities.

And there are a lot of them. You can visit Fiesta Island and go jetskiing. Sea World, whose star is Shamu the Killer Whale, offers some excellent exhibits and marine entertainment. The shark exhibits, penguin environment, and bat ray pool are hit attractions.

If you want to get out on the water, you can stop at one of the many marinas and rent a boat of any size—from paddleboat to oceangoing sloop.

The water areas of Mission Bay are organized, with areas set aside for jetskiing, waterskiing, sailing, hydroplanes, small sailboats, and large racing boats. This seems a big regimental, but it makes the visit even more pleasant.

Other attractions in the park include numerous jogging trails, fishing, hotels, golf courses, and a small amusement park.

North of Mission Bay Park is La Jolla and its great coves, beaches, and fine shops. For more information about this elegant and entertaining area, see Chapter One.

Downtown

San Diego is graced by a magnificent urban park with fine museums, a fine center city shopping complex, and two historic districts (one Spanish, the other a restored gaslight area near the waterfront).

Horton Plaza, a six-block area bounded by First and Fourth, Broadway and G streets, is a colorful and busy complex of shops, galleries, theaters, and restaurants. It's the anchor of San Diego's newest restoration effort, the Gaslamp Quarter.

The 16-block National Historic District was the center of commerce in San Diego in the 1800s. Its many Victorian buildings, shops, and warehouses fell into disuse in the 1900s, and it wasn't until 1974 that the value of the elegant and ornate buildings was recognized.

The district today is a haven for art galleries, restaurants, and shops, even though renovation is still continuing. The Gaslight Quarters Association, located in a nineteenth-century saltbox home (410 Island Avenue), conducts tours of the historic district Saturdays at 10 AM and 1 PM.

The century-plus buildings in the Gaslamp Quarter are mere babes compared to the structures in Old Town, which celebrates the area's Spanish and Mexican past.

Old Town is a state historic park, an area of about seven blocks bounded by Wallace, Congress, Juan, and Twigg streets. It was here in 1774 that Father Serra moved his mission, forced away from his first site near the bay by the need for fresh water and more room.

The mission is long gone, but it and the first settlers are remembered at Presidio Park, at Jackson and Twigg streets two blocks north of Old Town. The park contains the Serra Museum, a white-stucco and red-tile-roof structure with exhibits on the area's history since the mission days, and ruins of the first fort and the Spanish buildings.

Old Town sights include the Bazaar del Mundo, a shopping and dining area meant to look like a Mexican square; the Whaley House, at San Diego and Linwood streets, believed to be the oldest brick structure in southern California; the El Campo Santo, a 150-year-old adobe-walled cemetery that is also at San Diego and Linwood; and Casa de Estudillo, on Mason east of San Diego, the home of the commandante of Monterey and San Diego.

The Seeley Stables and barns at Juan and Twiggs were owned by the operator of a stagecoach line in the 1860s, while the Casa de Bandini, on Mason Street east of San Diego Street, grew from a one-story adobe to a two-story house when it became a stagecoach stop. Kit Carson is said to have visited here. It's now a restaurant.

Heritage Park, at Juan and Harney streets next to Old Town, is a small district with six houses representing San Diego's Victorian past. The houses are open daily from 9:30 AM to 5 PM.

These historic areas are not all of the center-city attractions in San Diego. For antique buffs, the neighborhood of Kensington has an antique row on Adams Street. More than two dozen dealers sell furniture, collectibles, and glasswares. Hillcrest, located off Route 163 east of the center of the city, has a number of interesting streets. Fourth and Fifth streets and University Avenue have cafes, theaters, bookstores, fine restaurants, and interesting shops.

The final major downtown attraction is one of the finest urban parks in the nation. Balboa Park is a 1,400-acre wonderland with fine museums, beautiful gardens, and numerous recreation activities.

The century-old park is due north of downtown. The park was started in 1868, but didn't really become an exceptional park until the 1915 Panama-California International Exposition and the 1935 California-Pacific International Exposition contributed a number of ornate and interesting structures to the garden. Enter the park from either Sixth Avenue, Laurel Street, or Park Boulevard.

We prefer the Laurel Street Bridge entrance. It crosses a canyon and enters the park's El Prado, the main pedestrian mall. The first attraction at this entry route is the Museum of Man, with outstanding anthropological exhibits. Next to the Museum of Man is the Simon Edison Centre for the Performing Arts. It has three theaters and offers a wide variety of entertainment. Beyond the center are the Sculpture Gardens, with a cute cafe surrounded by art, and next, the San Diego Museum of Art. The museum's collection ranges from early Asian art to contemporary works.

Next to the art museum is the Timken Art Gallery, which features European masters. Across El Prado is the Botanical Gardens, the Victorian-style greenhouse that was built for the 1915 exposition. More than 500 varieties of orchids are on display here. The lily pond out front is filled with koi and serves as a backdrop for the frequent mimes and street performers entertaining in front of the gardens.

Beyond the gardens is the park visitor center; the Hall of Champions, devoted to sports memorabilia; the Museum of Photographic Arts, a fairly new (1983) museum exhibiting photography, with a basement gallery that houses the model trains of the San Diego Model Railroad Museum; the Natural History Museum; and finally the Rueben H. Fleet Space Theater and Science Center.

After these museums comes a rose garden and cactus grove. As if this were not enough, roads lead to even more attractions.

There's the Organ Pavilion and the 5,000-pipe Spreckels Organ, the largest outdoor organ in the world, the San Diego Aerospace Museum and International Aerospace Hall of Fame, the San Diego Automotive Museum, and finally the world-famous San Diego Zoo.

Obviously, a visit to Balboa Park could take a week or more to see everything. Whenever you visit, take time to enjoy the many peaceful gardens, fountains, ponds, and groves.

Sidetrips

The attractions in San Diego County seem endless. There are these sidetrips, though, that warrant serious consideration:

Encinitas, about 25 miles north of town via coast road S21, is a flower-growing center, with so many poinsettia fields that the hills turn red in early December.

The San Diego Wild Animal Park, on Highway 78 near San Pasqual about 40 miles north of San Diego, is home to more than 2,000 animals. The animals, many of them endangered species, roam freely on the park's 1,800 acres. Visitors view the beasts by taking a monorail train on a 5-mile ride around the preserve.

Rancho Bernardo, on Interstate 15 south of Escondido, is slowly maturing into an arts colony, with more than 40 artisans having shops and studios in the Mercado near the Interstate 15 exit.

Julian, high in the hills in the eastern part of the county, is a colorful gold-mining town. Main Street still has the false-front stores and wooden sidewalks. You can visit the George Washington Mine, the first mine operated during the 1869 gold strike, and tour the Eagle Mine, off C Street in the center of the city.

✪ SAN FRANCISCO

It's almost too perfect. The City (never call it Frisco) appears to have everything that makes a metropolitan area great: history, culture, eclectic architecture, ethnic diversity, temperate climate, quaint neighborhoods, great restaurants, stunning scenery, and a mindset that puts an emphasis on the art of living well.

It's an outstanding city to visit. Nowhere else can you find so many diverse and interesting attractions within walking distance of each other. Nowhere else are the vistas ever changing, as fog, sun, and clouds are always creating new stagesets and backdrops for familiar landmarks on land and water.

San Francisco can be toured on foot, by cable car, bus, or subway. For those who cannot live without a car, The City is fairly easy to drive (although rush hour and the hills can be challenging). Most areas have plenty of commercial parking. We have broken San Francisco and the Bay Area into these tours: the Downtown (which includes Union Square, Chinatown, Japantown, Nob Hill, and North Beach), the Waterfront, Golden Gate Park, and Sidetrips (attractions on the Pacific Coast and around the Bay).

Downtown

Union Square is the heart of downtown San Francisco. Named for the pro-Union rallies held here in the years before the Civil War, the square is a modest (2.6 acres) urban park offering street performers, occasional concerts and protests, and a perfect spot to orient yourself before starting a tour of the rest of the city.

It's best to think of San Francisco as a city of neighborhoods. North and east of Union Square are Chinatown, North Beach, and the financial district and its landmark, the Transamerica pyramid. The waterfront stretches from the busy commercial piers on the

Embarcadero east of Union Square to the more touristy shops, ferry landings, and restaurants on the northern waterfront. Japantown, the elegant mansions of Pacific Heights, Golden Gate Park, and other attractions are west of the square.

Union Square is at Powell and Geary streets. You can catch a cable car on Powell Street or walk south three blocks from the square to Powell and Market streets and the starting point for two of the cable car lines. Powell and Market is also where you will find Hallidie Plaza and the San Francisco Visitors Information Center, where you can get maps, brochures on attractions, and information about current events.

There are two worthy attractions in the area south of Market Street, a light industrial region dubbed "SoMa" that is now turning into an entertainment district. The Old San Francisco Mint is at Fifth and Mission streets while the Ansel Adams Center (250 Fourth Street) has five galleries of photographs, including one of Adams' works.

After touring SoMa, return to Union Square and browse through the fine shops around it. Gump's, Saks Fifth Avenue, Macy's, I. Magnin, Neiman Marcus, and Gucci put some elegance into an otherwise modest square.

At the park's east end is Maiden Lane, a modest, two-block-long street that hosted many of the city's brothels until they were destroyed in the 1906 earthquake and fire.

The shops and offices that now occupy Maiden Lane are in sharp contrast to the street's scandalous past. After strolling the lane, turn north on Grant Avenue, which cuts across Maiden Lane, and head to Chinatown, a 24-block area where more than 100,000 Chinese live in the largest Chinese community outside of Asia.

Your first stop is at Grant Avenue and Bush Street and the Chinatown Gate, a green-tile portal that is the entryway to an exotic neighborhood filled with unusual sights, smells, and sounds. Grant Avenue, Stockton Street a block west, and the other streets of Chinatown are filled with restaurants, food stores, and shops. While much of the merchandise sold is garish and useless, the shops are interesting.

Turn east and walk to Kearny Street and continue north to the Pacific Heritage Museum, in the Bank of Canton (608 Commercial Street), just north of the intersection of Kearny and Sacramento streets. Another block north is the Holiday Inn (750 Kearny), where you will find the Chinese Culture Center and its exhibits of Chinese art and crafts.

Continue north to Montgomery Street and turn left to 743 and the colorful three-tiered pagoda that is the Old Chinese Telephone exchange. It was built in 1909.

Other attractions in Chinatown include the Chinese Historical Society (17 Adler Place) near Grant and Columbus avenues, the Tien Hou Temple (125 Waverly Place) near Stockton and Clay streets, and Portsmouth Square at Kearny and Clay streets. The square is where Captain John B. Montgomery raised the American flag in 1846, claiming the Mexican village on this location as a possession of the United States.

The square is marked by a 9-foot granite shaft erected in 1919 and dedicated to the memory of writer Robert Louis Stevenson, who often visited the park when he lived in the city in 1879–80.

Chinatown slowly gives way to the next neighborhood—North Beach, known as a haven for the Beat movement of the 1950s but an area whose heart and soul have remained firmly and passionately Italian since the first Genoese fisherman settled here in the early 1840s.

Columbus Avenue is the lifeline of North Beach. Along this boulevard you will find Washington Square, the center of the enclave. The five-sided square at Columbus and Union Street is a popular socializing spot for elderly Italian men. The square is anchored by the Romanesque Church of Saints Peter and Paul on Filbert. The twin terra-cotta towers are landmarks.

Cafes and coffeehouses are popular social centers in North Beach. Caffe Puccini (411 Columbus), Caffe Roma (414 Columbus), and Caffe Trieste (601 Vallejo Street) are wonderful places to stop for an espresso and watch the passing parade. Grant Avenue north of Columbus is another area lined with cafes, restaurants, and galleries.

North Beach has many unusual shops. Try visiting Quantity Postcards (1441 Grant Avenue), where more than 10,000 different cards—old and new—can be bought. The Beat movement was born in North Beach in the 1950s. Most of the Beatniks and their followers have moved on, but the movement's passion still burns brightly at poet Lawrence Ferlinghetti's City Lights Bookstore (261 Columbus Avenue). Ferlinghetti has offices in a nearby building but still occasionally holds court at the store.

The best view in town is a few minutes walk from Columbus Avenue. Telegraph Hill, at Filbert and Kearny streets, is topped by the Coit Tower, a popular subject for photographers. Take the steps from Filbert Street up the 300-foot hill to the 210-foot-high tower, which is a monument to the city's firefighters. Between 11 AM and 5 PM, you can take an elevator to the top of the tower, where you can see the Golden Gate and Bay bridges, the waterfront, Alcatraz, Nob Hill, and many areas of the city. The tower is decorated with murals painted by 25 artists. Pioneer Park at the foot of the tower is popular with painters seeking inspiration from the incredible vista.

Another city high spot is Russian Hill, notable for its mix of quaint cottages and high-rise apartment buildings and what is called the most crooked street in the world, Lombard Street. A steep brick road between Hyde and Leavenworth streets, it twists and turns as it passes flower gardens and fancy townhomes. Walking or driving it is an adventure.

The wealth and power of San Francisco can be seen in two neighborhoods west of Chinatown and North Beach. Nob Hill, at Sacramento and Taylor streets, is where San Francisco's wealthiest families built their estates and where four of the city's best hotels—Stanford Court, Mark Hopkins, Huntington, and Fairmont—are located. Grace Cathedral, at California and Taylor, is the third largest Episcopal cathedral in the nation and one of the finest examples of gothic architecture in the country. (The California and Powell street cable car lines cross Nob Hill, so access is fairly easy.)

Pacific Heights is the domain of the superrich. Pacific Heights is bounded roughly by Van Ness Street on the east, California Street on the south, the Presidio on the west, and the Bay to the north. Within this neighborhood are million-dollar mansions, lavish consulates, grand Victorians, elegant Queen Annes, and stately Georgians. The oldest and grandest often trace their birth to the gold rush days. Comstock mine heir James Flood built the Italian Renaissance palace at 2222 Broadway, and William Bourn, who owned the Mother Lode gold mine, built the Georgian mansion at 2550 Webster Street.

Another luxurious estate is the California Historical Society, located in a huge red sandstone mansion (2090 Jackson Street). A block east of the society's building is the 1800 block of Laguna, where beautiful Italianate Victorians line the street. Another formal estate is the Spreckels Palace (2080 Washington Street). It was built by sugar heir Adolph Spreckels.

While these homes remain closed to the public, one mansion allows a glimpse into the lifestyle of the 1880s. The Haas-Lilienthal mansion (2007 Franklin) was built in 1886. The Queen

Anne structure is fully furnished with magnificent Victorian antiques and tours are offered from noon to 4 PM Wednesday, 11 AM to 4:30 PM Sunday. Call 415/441-3004.

Another downtown attraction we like to visit is Japantown, a neighborhood where 12,000 Japanese-Americans live. Japantown is anchored by the Japan Center at Post and Buchanan streets. The center is a 5-acre complex of shops, restaurants, galleries, sushi bars, and a five-tiered pagoda flanked by a plaza with traditional Japanese gardens and reflecting pools.

After a busy day of touring, the Peace Plaza is a perfect place to rest.

The Waterfront

The north waterfront is the most picturesque area of The City. Here you will find fine seafood restaurants, ferries to take you around the picturesque bay, and century-old industrial blocks converted to shops, art galleries, and restaurants.

The most entertaining way to go to the northern waterfront is by cable car. The quaint and noisy cable cars are a national monument, the only such monument that moves. If you want to go to the waterfront, catch a car on the Powell-Hyde line at Union Square and take it north to the end of the line.

The cable car stops a few blocks from the waterfront. Two blocks west of the car terminus is the Aquatic Park, where the views of the Bay and Bridge are great when the weather is nice. The National Maritime Museum at the park and Polk Street examines San Francisco's maritime past and has a number of fine ship models.

On the eastern edge of the park is the Hyde Street Pier, where several century-old historic ships are berthed. These include the

C. A. Thayer, a three-masted schooner, and the Eureka, a side-wheel ferry. You can tour the ships for a small fee.

On the south side of the Aquatic Park is Ghiradelli Square, a nineteenth-century brick factory that made chocolate until the 1960s. Now the renovated industrial area is home to many fine shops, restaurants, and galleries.

More shopping and dining temptations can be found east of the Hyde Street Pier at the Cannery, a century-old Del Monte canning factory.

Stroll along Jefferson Street and the waterfront to pier 45 and Fisherman's Wharf. The fishing fleet, a wide selection of seafood restaurants, souvenir vendors, and street performers—mimes, magicians, and once even a "human jukebox"—offer entertaining and interesting diversions.

At pier 41 farther east on the waterfront, you can catch the Red and White Fleet ferries to Alcatraz, Sausalito, and sightseeing around the Bay and under the Golden Gate Bridge.

The other waterfront attractions are on the western end of the marine district. At Baker and Beach streets is the Palace of Fine Arts, the only structure still standing from the 1915 Panama-Pacific Exposition. The columned rotunda and lake with swans is a romantic and beautiful setting for a picnic or brief rest stop. The Palace holds the Exploratorium, a science museum with many hands-on exhibits.

Just west of the Palace is the Presidio, the 1,500-acre headquarters of the U.S. Sixth Army. The Presidio has been a military post for more than 200 years. The Spanish had a fort there, and were succeeded by the Mexicans and finally Americans.

Just south of the Presidio is another fine shopping area. Sacramento Street, between Broderick and Spruce streets, is home to Sue Fisher King (Florentine linens; 3067 Sacramento),

Virginia Breier (West Coast crafts; 3091 Sacramento), Robert Hering & Associates (antiques; 3307 Sacramento), Sante Fe (Southwestern art and crafts; 3571 Sacramento), and other shops and bistros.

If you have a car, drive down Lincoln Boulevard into the Presidio to Long Avenue and Fort Point. The Point is just east and under the Golden Gate Bridge. If you don't have a car, you can reach the point by walking west from the Aquatic Park the 3.5 miles along the Golden Gate Promenade.

However you get to Fort Point, the views of the Bay, the Bridge, and the City are incredible. It's a great place to picnic or just watch the fog roll in.

Golden Gate Park

This 1,000-acre oasis is a delight. You can drive, bike, hike, or jog the roads, enjoy a Sunday concert, play tennis, softball, or soccer, ride a horse, or stroll through the city's finest museums.

John F. Kennedy Drive takes you to most of the attractions in the park. Start at the east end of the park by visiting the Conservatory, an elaborate Victorian greenhouse that is a copy of Kew Gardens in London. The Conservatory has a tropical garden and seasonal displays of plants and flowers.

Continue west on the drive to the M. H. de Young Memorial Museum, which has 44 galleries of art. While the focus is on American artists, the museum has an extensive collection of African, Asian, and Mediterranean works. The Avery Brundage Collection of Oriental Art, displaying more than 6,000 pieces of art covering 60 centuries, overlooks the Japanese Tea Garden. The garden is a 4-acre fantasyland of bridges, ponds, flowering plants, and serene meadows.

Southeast of the de Young museum, across the Music Concourse, is the California Academy of Sciences, which features an outstanding aquarium holding more than 14,000 fish, a room that simulates an earthquake, and other exhibits on man and his habitat.

The Music Concourse is the setting for band concerts at 2 PM Sundays and holidays, weather permitting.

South of the Tea Garden are two beautiful gardens: the Shakespeare Garden, which displays more than 200 flowers and plants mentioned in the writings of the Bard, and the Strybing Arboretum, with gardens of more than 6,000 plants common to the area.

Continue west in the park to Stow Lake and the boathouse where you can rent a paddleboat for a cruise on the waters. The Chinese Pavilion on the island in the lake was a gift from Taipei.

Farther west are the stables, at 34th Avenue and Kennedy Drive. You can rent a horse there. Bicycles can be rented from vendors stationed just outside the park in the 600 and 800 blocks of Stanyan Street.

Kennedy Drive continues west, passing more lakes, the Buffalo Meadow where these animals may be seen living in peace, and the 1902 Dutch Windmill and Queen Wilhelmina Tulip Garden. The last two attractions are in the extreme northwest end of the park, where the drive merges with the Great Highway.

The park ends at this bluff above the Pacific shore. You can drive the Great Highway a mile north to Lincoln Park and Land's End, a seafront point with spectacular views of Marin County and the Golden Gate Bridge. The park is also home to the California Palace of the Legion of Honor, an excellent museum with sculptures by Rodin, Anna Huntington, French and European decorative arts and furnishings, and paintings by Rembrandt, El Greco, Manet, Titian, Degas, and Cezanne.

One of our rituals of visiting San Francisco is a stop at Cliff

✪ The Golden Gate Bridge, one of the more famous spans in the world. (Courtesy of the San Francisco Convention & Visitors Bureau)

House (1066 Point Lobos Avenue) just south of Lincoln Park. Cliff House is a restaurant, gift shop, and museum of antique mechanical devices (Musée Mécanique is the unlikely name of the place).

We visit Cliff House not for the food or antique nickelodeons.

Our destination is two levels below, on the sightseeing platform, where you will find an observation deck and the Golden Gate National Recreation Area Visitors Center. From the deck, you can look out at the cute barking sea lions on Seal Rocks.

South of Cliff House is Ocean Beach, a great place for surfside walks but not the place to swim. The surf is unsafe. Farther south are two other attractions. The San Francisco Zoo is at Sloat Boulevard and the Great Highway, and past the animals is Fort Funston, which has some great hiking trails with spectacular views and the favorite launching site of hang gliders.

These man-piloted wings are a colorful and breathtaking sight. It's a perfect way to end a day filled with beauty.

Around the Bay

The San Francisco Bay Area offers several other attractions, all easily reached by car or ferry from The City.

Sausalito (described in Chapter Three) is a popular day trip. You can drive to Sausalito by taking Highway 1/101 over the Golden Gate Bridge. A more pleasant and scenic trip is by taking the Red and White Fleet ferries from pier 41 at Fisherman's Wharf (415/546-2896) or the Golden Gate Ferry from the Ferry Building at Market Street and the Embarcadero (415/332-6600). The trips take less than a half-hour, and Sausalito is a fun town with numerous art galleries, restaurants, and fine shops.

Oakland, on the eastern shore of the Bay, is a large city with a number of fine attractions. The Oakland Museum (100 Oak Street) has exhibits on the history, art, and nature wonders of California. Behind the museum is Lake Merritt, a 155-acre lake with parkland and paths. The lake is a wildfowl refuge.

On Oakland's Inner Harbor, at the foot of Broadway, is Jack London Square, a 10-block area with many restaurants and saloons. Jack London Village next door has many fine shops.

✪ FOR MORE INFORMATION

Beverly Hills Visitors Bureau. 239 South Beverly Drive, Beverly Hills, CA 90212. 213/271-8174 and 800/345-2210 nationwide.

Hollywood Chamber of Commerce. 6255 Sunset Boulevard, Suite 911, Hollywood, CA 90028. 213/469-8311.

Julian Chamber of Commerce. Main and Washington streets, P.O. Box 413, Julian, CA 92036. 619/765-1857.

Los Angeles Convention and Visitors Bureau. 515 South Figueroa Street, 11th Floor, Los Angeles, CA 90071. 213/624-7300.

Oakland Convention and Visitors Bureau. 1000 Broadway, Suite 200, Oakland, CA 94607-4020. 415/839-9000 and 800/444-7270 nationwide.

San Diego Visitors Information Center, 2688 East Mission Bay Drive, San Diego, CA 92109. 619/276-8200.

San Francisco Convention and Visitors Bureau. 201 Third Street, Suite 900, San Francisco, CA 94103-3185. 415/974-6900.

Santa Monica Visitors Center. 400 Ocean Avenue, Santa Monica, CA 90401. 213/393-7593.

✪ WHERE AND WHEN

Los Angeles

Craft and Folk Art Museum. 5814 Wilshire Boulevard, Los Angeles. Open 11 AM to 5 PM Tuesday through Sunday. Closed Monday. 213/937-5544.

J. Paul Getty Museum. 17985 Pacific Coast Highway, Malibu. Open

10 AM to 5 PM Tuesday through Sunday. Reservations required for parking. 213/458-2003.

Hollyhock House. In Bransdall Park, 4800 Hollywood Boulevard, Hollywood. Tours on the hour from 10 AM to 1 PM Tuesday through Thursday, noon to 3 PM Saturdays and the first three Sundays of the month. 213/662-7272.

Hollywood Bowl. 2301 North Highland Avenue, Los Angeles. Call 213/850-2000 for the schedule of entertainment.

Huntington Library, Art Collection, and Botanical Gardens. 1151 Oxford Road, San Marino. Open 1 PM to 4:30 PM Tuesday through Sunday. Reservations required Sunday. 818/405-2100.

Los Angeles Museum of Contemporary Art. 250 South Grand Avenue. Open 11 AM to 6 PM Tuesday through Wednesday and weekends, 11 AM to 8 PM Thursday. 213/626-6222.

Mann's Chinese Theatre. 6925 Hollywood Boulevard, Hollywood. Open daily. 213/461-3331.

Norton Simon Museum of Art. 411 West Colorado Boulevard, Pasadena. Open noon to 6 PM Thursday through Sunday. 818/449-3730.

Olvera Street. West 17th Street and Olvera Street, Los Angeles. The Mexican marketplace is open 10 AM to 10 PM in summer, 10 AM to 7:30 PM in the winter. 213/628-4349.

Pacific Asia Museum. 46 North Los Robles Avenue, Pasadena. Open noon to 5 PM Wednesday through Sunday. Tours at 2 PM Sunday. 818/449-2742.

George C. Page Museum of La Brea Discoveries. 5801 Wilshire

Boulevard, Los Angeles. Open 10 AM to 5 PM Tuesday through Sunday. 213/936-2230.

El Pueblo de Los Angeles. 845 North Alameda Street, Los Angeles. Open 10 AM to 10 PM in summer, 10 AM to 7:30 PM in winter. 213/628-1274.

Santa Monica Heritage Museum. 2612 Main Street, Santa Monica. Open 11 AM to 4 PM Thursday through Saturday, noon to 4 PM Sunday. 213/392-8537.

Santa Monica Museum of Art. 2437 Main Street, Santa Monica. Open 11 AM to 8 PM Wednesday through Thursday, 11 AM to 6 PM Friday through Sunday. 213/399-0433.

Santa Monica Pier. Ocean and Colorado avenues, Santa Monica. Open 10 AM to 9 PM Tuesday through Sunday in the summer, 10 AM to 5 PM weekends in the winter. 213/394-7554.

San Diego

Aerospace Museum. 2001 Pan America Plaza. Open 10 AM to 4:30 PM daily. 619/234-8291.

Cabrillo National Monument (Point Loma). Route 209. Open 9 AM to 5:15 PM daily. 619/557-5450.

Simon Edison Center for the Performing Arts. Balboa Park. Call 619/239-2255 for the schedule of entertainment.

Reuben H. Fleet Space Theater and Science Center. El Prado, Balboa Park. Open 9:30 AM to 9:30 PM daily. 619/238-1233.

Heritage Park. 2455 Heritage Park Row. Open 9:30 AM to 5 PM daily. 619/565-5928.

Horton Plaza. 324 Horton Plaza. Open 10 AM to 9 PM weekdays, 10 AM to 6 PM Saturday, 11 AM to 6 PM Sunday. 619/239-8180.

Maritime Museum. 1306 North Harbor Drive. Open 9 AM to 8 PM daily. 619/234-9153.

Old Town. 4002 Wallace Street. Open daily. 619/237-6770.

San Diego Museum of Art. El Prado, Balboa Park. Open 10 AM to 4:30 PM Tuesday through Sunday. 619/232-7931.

San Diego Museum of Man. El Prado, Balboa Park. Open 10 AM to 4:30 PM daily. 619/239-2001.

San Diego Wild Animal Park. 15500 San Pasqual Valley Road, Escondido. Open 9 AM to dusk daily. 619/747-8702.

San Diego Zoo. Balboa Park. Open 9 AM to 4 PM September through June, 9 AM to 5 PM July through Labor Day. 619/557-3966.

Sea World. 1720 South Shores Road. Open 9 AM to dusk daily. 619/335-1184.

Serra Museum. Presidio Park. Open 10 AM to 4:30 PM Tuesday through Saturday, noon to 4:30 PM Sunday. 619/297-3258.

San Francisco

Alcatraz Island. Guided and self-guided tours of this national park. 415/546-2896.

Asian Art Museum. Golden Gate Park. Open 10 AM to 5 PM Wednesday through Sunday. 415/668-8921.

Cable Car Museum. Washington and Mason streets. Open 10 AM to 6 PM daily. 415/474-1887.

California Academy of Sciences. Golden Gate Park. Open 10 AM to 5 PM daily. 415/750-7145.

California Historical Society. 2090 Jackson Street. Open 1 PM to 4:30 PM Wednesday through Sunday. 415/567-1848.

Coit Tower. Telegraph Hill. Open 10 AM to 5:30 PM daily June through September, 9 AM to 4:30 PM daily October through May. 415/362-8037.

Conservatory of Flowers. Golden Gate Park. Open 9 AM to 6 PM daily. 415/558-3973.

M. H. de Young Memorial Museum. Golden Gate Park. Open 10 AM to 5 PM daily. 415/750-3600.

Exploratorium/Palace of Fine Arts. 3601 Lyon Street. Open 10 AM to 5 PM Wednesday through Sunday. 415/561-0360.

Oakland Museum. 1000 Oak Street, Oakland. Open 10 AM to 5 PM Wednesday through Saturday, noon to 7 PM Sunday. 415/834-2413.

Old Mint. Fifth and Mission streets. Open 10 AM to 4 PM weekdays. 415/744-6830.

Palace of the Legion of Honor. Lincoln Park. Open 10 AM to 5 PM Wednesday through Sunday. 415/750-3600.

Presidio. Museum open 10 AM to 4 PM Tuesday through Sunday. 415/556-1693.

San Francisco Zoo. Sloat Boulevard and 45th Avenue. Open 10 AM to 5 PM daily. 415/661-2023.

✪ ROMANTIC RETREATS

Los Angeles, San Diego, and San Francisco are not the places to find cheap hotels and restaurants. And there are other differences. Los Angeles is the place to find big, elegant hotels, while San Francisco has scores of fine inns in historic buildings. And San Diego is a bit of both, with some nice inns as well as large hotels.

Here are our favorite places, but first an explanation of how we break down our cost categories:

One night in a hotel, resort, or inn for two:

Inexpensive	Less than $100
Moderate	$100 to $150
Expensive	More than $150

Dinner for two (drinks not included):

Inexpensive	Less than $30
Moderate	$30 to $75
Expensive	More than $75

Los Angeles: Romantic Lodging

✪ *Le Bel Age Hotel.* Elegant suites make this all-suite hotel in West Hollywood an outstanding retreat. There are 190 suites, many with terraces with great views of the city. Facilities include a pool. Expensive. 1020 North San Vicente Boulevard, West Hollywood, CA 90069. 213/854-1111 and 800/424-4443 nationwide.

✪ *Bel Air.* Small, secluded, and surrounded by beautiful gardens, this 38-room and 32-suite hotel offers splendid accommodations. Expensive. 701 Stone Canyon Road, Bel Air, CA 90077. 213/472-1211 and 800/648-4097 nationwide.

✪ *Beverly Hills Hotel.* This is a beautiful landmark known for its magnificent grounds, its celebrity-studded Polo Lounge, and its 331 beautifully furnished rooms. The bungalows are preferred by stars seeking seclusion, a trysting spot, and the hotel's discretion. Facilities include a pool and exercise room. Expensive. 9641 Sunset Boulevard, Beverly Hills, CA 90210. 213/276-2251 and 800/283-8885 nationwide.

✪ *Beverly House Hotel.* Small but elegant, this 50-room hotel is run like a bed-and-breakfast. Moderate. 140 South Lasky Dr., Beverly Hills, CA 90212. 213/271-2145 and 800/432-5444 nationwide.

✪ *The Biltmore.* This historic landmark has hosted many Hollywood notables since it opened in 1923. Mary Pickford, J. Paul Getty, U.S. presidents, and visiting royalty have found the hotel is a beautiful gem. The lobby is Italian, with a painted ceiling and lots of Italian marble. The 704 rooms have recently been refurbished and now offer all modern conveniences and tasteful furnishings. Facilities include a health club. Expensive. 506 South Grand Avenue, Los Angeles, CA 90013. 213/624-1011 and 800/245-8673 nationwide.

✪ *Century Plaza Hotel.* Surrounded by colorful gardens of exotic plants and pools, this huge (1,072 rooms) hotel features 20- and 30-story towers, spacious rooms with great views, and 2 pools. Expensive. 2025 Avenue of the Stars, Century City, CA 90067. 213/277-2000 and 800/228-3000 nationwide.

✪ *Chateau Marmount.* Despite its location amid the garish commercialism of the Sunset Strip, this Normandy-style hotel still maintains a classy ambiance while offering privacy to its prominent guests. There are 62 rooms in the hotel, bungalows, and fully equipped cottages. Facilities include a pool and gardens. Expensive. 8221 Sunset Boulevard, West Hollywood, CA 90046. 213/656-1010 and 800/CHATEAU nationwide.

✪ *Checkers.* Another historic hotel, but smaller and more sedate than the Biltmore. The 190 rooms in this 65-year-old landmark are spacious and nicely furnished. Facilities include a rooftop pool and exercise studio. Expensive. 535 South Grand Avenue, Los Angeles, CA 90071. 213/624-0000 and 800/628-4900 nationwide.

✪ *Eastlake Inn.* This lovely 1887 Eastlake-style inn has eight nice rooms, all furnished with antiques and some with fireplaces. Two of the rooms have private baths. Moderate/expensive. 1442 Kellam Avenue, Los Angeles, CA 90026. 213/250-1620.

✪ *L'Ermitage Hotel.* One of the finest hotels in the nation, this luxurious 114-room combines European style with modern necessities. The suites are particularly wonderful, with fireplaces and sunken living rooms. Facilities include a pool and spa. Expensive. 9291 Burton Way, Beverly Hills, CA 90201. 213/278-3344 and 800/424-4443 nationwide.

✪ *Four Seasons.* Close to the shops of Rodeo Drive, this new European-style hotel exudes class. But what would you expect of a Four Seasons property? There are 285 spacious and nicely furnished rooms. Facilities include a pool and exercise room. Expensive. 300 South Doheny Drive, Beverly Hills, CA 90048. 213/273-2222 and 800/332-3442 nationwide.

✿ *Hyatt on Sunset.* Popular with music industry figures, including a few recording stars, this Hyatt offers 262 spacious and tastefully decorated rooms. Facilities include a pool. Expensive. 8401 West Sunset Boulevard, Hollywood, CA 90069. 213/656-4101 and 800/223-1234 nationwide.

✿ *Loews Santa Monica Beach Hotel.* Close to the shops on Main Street and the wide beach, this new contemporary-design hotel offers fine rooms. Facilities include a pool, health club, and private access to the beach. Expensive. 1700 Ocean Avenue, Santa Monica, CA 90401. 213/458-6700 and 800/223-0888 nationwide.

✿ *Ma Maison Sofitel Hotel.* The location is great—close to the fine shops and restaurants of Beverly Hills—and the rooms are large and beautifully decorated in country French. Facilities include a pool, sauna, and fitness center. Expensive. 855 Beverly Road, Beverly Hills, CA 90048. 213/278-5444 and 800/221-4542 nationwide.

✿ *The New Otani and Gardens.* As its name implies, this is a Japanese-owned hotel that blends the fine touches of Nippon with western flash. There are 448 spacious and well-equipped rooms in the 21-story tower surrounded by waterfalls, ponds, and gardens. Facilities include sauna and massage. Expensive. 120 South Figueroa Street, Los Angeles, CA 90012. 213/629-1200; and 800/252-0197 in California, 800/421-8795 elsewhere in the United States.

✿ *Regent Beverly Wilshire.* Made famous by the movie *Pretty Woman,* this low-key luxury hotel offers class, style, and 453 excellent rooms. The location is tops, too. Rodeo Drive is right outside. Facilities include a pool and spa. Expensive. 9500 Wilshire Boulevard, Beverly Hills, CA 90212. 213/275-4282 and 800/421-4354 nationwide.

✪ *Ritz-Carlton Hotels.* There are two new Ritz-Carltons in the Los Angeles area. In Marina del Rey, the high-rise Ritz offers 306 stylish rooms overlooking the coast and marinas. Facilities include a pool. Expensive. 4200 Admiralty Way, Marina del Rey, CA 90292. 213/823-3656. The other new Ritz-Carlton is in Pasadena at the renovated Huntington Hotel. The refurbished hotel has 385 magnificent rooms and 6 cottages. It is surrounded by restored Japanese gardens originally designed in 1911. Facilities include a pool and fitness center. Expensive. 1401 South Oak Knoll Avenue, Pasadena, CA 91106. 818/568-3160.

✪ *Saint James's Club.* One of the chain of luxury St. James's Clubs, this 63-room hotel re-creates the 1930s with replica art deco furnishings, a 1930s-ish supper club, and other touches. Facilities include a pool, sauna, and health center. Expensive. 8358 Sunset Boulevard, West Hollywood, CA 90069. 213/654-7100 and 800/225-2637 nationwide.

✪ *Salisbury House.* Located in a quiet neighborhood near USC, this 1909 Craftsman has five nicely furnished rooms. Three of the rooms have private baths. Moderate. 2273 West 20th Street, Los Angeles, CA 90018. 213/737-7817 and 800/373-1778 nationwide.

✪ *Westin Bonaventure.* The views are striking from the 1,474 rooms in this 35-story circular highrise. The rooms are spacious and nicely decorated, the gardens and waterfalls are in the lobby, and the outside elevators can be thrilling. Facilities include a pool and five levels of shops. Expensive. Fifth and Figueroa streets, Los Angeles, CA 90071. 213/624-1000 and 800/228-3000 nationwide.

Los Angeles: Fine Dining

For fine dining in Los Angeles, the choices seem limitless. The superstars—Matsuhisa, Spago's, Chinois on Main, Fennel, Valentino—require reservations far in advance. Here are our choices:

❂ *Angeli Mare.* Rustic Italian cooking featuring fresh seafood. Moderate. 13455 Maxella Avenue, Marina del Rey. 213/822-1984.

❂ *Babette's.* This pleasant Marina del Rey restaurant is a great place for lunch or dinner on the patio when the weather is nice. The cuisine is Californian, featuring great salads and creative meat dishes. Expensive. 3100 Washington Boulevard, Marina del Rey. 213/822-2020.

❂ *Bel Air Hotel.* Excellent continental cuisine served with Californian touches in this romantic room set amid the gardens. Expensive. 701 Stone Canyon Road, Bel Air. 213/472-1211.

❂ *Chasen's.* Once it was the place to be and be seen in, and now this American fare restaurant still serves outstanding dishes. Expensive. 9039 Beverly Boulevard, West Hollywood. 213/271-2168.

❂ *Chaya Venice.* The newest of three Chaya restaurants in L.A. (there are more in France and Italy), this excellent and innovative restaurant blends the cuisines of Japan, France, Italy, and California into everchanging surprises. The best dishes are seafood, particularly the ginger-marinated 'ahi tuna and the paella (although we draw the line at flavoring the rice with squid ink). Moderate. 110 Navy Street, Venice. 213/396-1179.

❂ *Checker's.* Superb Californian-American cuisine served in a clubby room. Moderate. 535 South Grand Avenue, Los Angeles. 213/624-0000.

❂ *Chinois on Main.* Another Wolfgang Puck creation, this time where Peking meets Paris, both on the menu and in the unusual decor. The food is excellent, offering creations from catfish with ginger to Mongolian lamb. Expensive. 2709 Main Street, Santa Monica. 213/392-9025.

✪ *Citrus*. Exquisite Californian-French cuisine, created by one of the nation's greatest chefs, Michel Richard. Expensive. 6703 Melrose Avenue, West Hollywood. 213/857-0034.

✪ *The Dining Room*. Outstanding Californian cuisine served in a European salon at the marvelous Regent Beverly Wilshire. Expensive. 9500 Wilshire Boulevard, Beverly Hills. 213/275-5200.

✪ *Dynasty Room*. The Sunday brunch is the superstar at this fine continental restaurant in the Westwood Marquis Hotel. Moderate. 930 Hilgard Avenue, Westwood. 213/208-9765.

✪ *Empress Pavilion*. One of the new restaurants in Chinatown, this dining room features a wide-ranging menu, with excellent dim sum and classic Cantonese dishes. The savory veal rolls, Peking duck, and baked oysters are superb. Moderate. 988 North Hill Street, in the Bamboo Plaza. 213/617-9898.

✪ *Engine Co. #28*. This restored landmark serves American classics. We like the chili and the grilled fish. Moderate. Figueroa Street and Wilshire Boulevard, Los Angeles. 213/624-6996.

✪ *L'Ermitage*. Outstanding Californian-French in a countrylike setting at this fabulous hotel. Expensive. 730 North La Cienega Boulevard, West Hollywood. 213/652-5840.

✪ *Eureka*. Another fine creation by Wolfgang Puck (Spago, Chinois on Main). This exciting restaurant built around a microbrewery features bratwurst and weisswurst as well as Chinese-almond duck sausage, spice-smoked salmon, Grandma Puck's cheese ravioli, and other delights. Expensive. 1845 South Bundy Drive. 213/447-8000.

✪ *Fennel.* Parisian cooking that will make your heart soar. Expensive. 1535 Ocean Avenue, Santa Monica. 213/394-2079.

✪ *Killer Shrimp.* Shrimp-lovers rejoice. You have a choice of boiled shrimp or boiled shrimp with bread. Either way it's a great place for lunch. Inexpensive. 523 Washington Boulevard, Marina del Rey. 213/578-2293.

✪ *Mandarin.* Great Chinese food in a setting that would do honors to a fine French restaurant. Moderate. 430 North Camden Drive, Beverly Hills. 213/272-0267.

✪ *Jody Maroni's Italian Sausage Kingdom.* The best of the wursts, with sausages unlike any you have seen. Try the Yucatan duck with cumin, the curried lamb, or the spicy Italian. The sausages are served on a soft roll with onions. Inexpensive. 2011 Ocean Front Walk, Venice. 213/306-1995.

✪ *Matsuhisa.* Acclaimed by many as the finest restaurant in Los Angeles, this innovative dining room features an exciting and surprising marriage of Japanese cuisine, sushi, and Latin cuisines. Expensive. 129 North La Cienega Boulevard, Hollywood. 213/659-9639.

✪ *North Beach Bar and Grill.* Excellent and creative Californian cuisine. The chili was great, as was the seafood. Sunday brunch is even better. The beautiful bar and aquarium invite you to relax for a drink before a meal. Don't miss the 35-foot-tall moving kewpie doll on the facade. Moderate. Rose Avenue and Main Street, Venice. 213/399-3900.

✪ *L'Orangerie.* A beautiful, elegant dining room and superb French cuisine. Expensive. 903 North La Cienega Boulevard, West Hollywood. 213/652-9770.

✪ *Rex-Il Ristorante.* One of the more beautiful restaurants in Los Angeles, this Italian dining room serves excellent seafood. Expensive. 617 South Olive Street. 213/627-2300.

✪ *Rockenwagner.* Outstanding French cuisine, at an always surprising restaurant. Moderate. 1023 Abbot Kinney Boulevard, Venice. 213/399-6504.

✪ *La Salsa.* They are everywhere in Los Angeles, and these haute Mexican fast-food outlets serve excellent food. Try them for lunch, for the decor is lacking any ambiance. Inexpensive. La Salsas are at 9311 Little Santa Monica Boulevard, Beverly Hills, 213/726-2273; 11075 West Pico Boulevard, Los Angeles, 213/479-0919; and other locations.

✪ *Seventh Street Bistro.* Nouvelle French-Californian cuisine served in an elegant art deco building. Moderate. 811 West Seventh Street, Los Angeles. 213/627-1242.

✪ *Spago.* Wolfgang Puck made this West Hollywood spot the place to be seen. Even without the star-studded clientele, Puck has created an outstanding menu, featuring grilled meats, fresh seafood, and innovative pizzas. Expensive. 1114 Horn Avenue, West Hollywood. 213/652-4025.

✪ *Trumps.* The setting is a modern adobe and the menu is very creative Californian. Moderate. 8764 Melrose Avenue, West Hollywood. 213/855-1480.

✪ *Valentino.* The finest Italian restaurant in Los Angeles. That says it all. Expensive. 3115 Pico Boulevard, Santa Monica. 213/829-4313.

✿ *West Beach Cafe.* Classic dishes meet haute California at this upscale spot in Venice. Moderate. 60 North Venice Boulevard, Venice. 213/823-5396.

San Diego: Romantic Lodging

✿ *Balboa Park Inn.* This bed-and-breakfast has 25 one- or two-bedroom suites, all furnished with antiques. Some suites have fireplaces and whirlpools. Expensive. 3402 Park Boulevard, San Diego, CA 92103. 619/298-0823.

✿ *Britt House.* This elegant 1887 Queen Anne near Balboa Park has 10 rooms, 2 with private baths. The furnishings are antique. Moderate. 406 Maple Street, San Diego, CA 92103. 619/234-2926.

✿ *Coronado Victorian House.* This beautiful 1894 Victorian has six antique-filled rooms. The room rates include dance and exercise classes. Expensive. 1000 Eighth Street, Coronado, CA 92118. 619/435-2200.

✿ *Doubletree Hotel.* The decor is Southwestern at this 350-room luxury high-rise hotel. Facilities include a pool, spa, and fitness center. Expensive. 901 Camino del Rio South, San Diego, CA 92108. 619/543-9000 and 800/528-0444 nationwide.

✿ *Glorietta Bay Inn.* Close to the Del and the harbor, this nice 100-room hotel is a fine alternative to the bigger, busier spots. Expensive. 1630 Glorietta Boulevard, Coronado, CA 92118. 619/435-3101.

✿ *U. S. Grant Hotel.* Built in 1910 and renovated and reopened in the 1980s, this majestic, formal hotel has 280 rooms and a great location in the center of the city. Expensive. 326 Broadway, San Diego, CA 92101. 619/232-3121.

❂ *Heritage Park Inn.* Lovely 1889 Queen Anne Victorian has nine rooms, five with private baths. The rooms are lovely and are furnished with antiques. Moderate. 2470 Heritage Park Row, San Diego, CA 92110. 619/295-7088.

❂ *Horton Grand Hotel.* The oldest Victorian hotel in the city, this recently restored 110-room hotel has cozy rooms furnished with period antiques. Expensive. 311 Island Avenue, San Diego, CA 92101. 619/544-1886.

❂ *Hotel del Coronado.* The grand dame of San Diego, this magnificent Victorian hotel should be seen if you cannot stay here. There are 700 rooms in the white-frame main house and the more modern additions. The rooms are spacious, and most have porches or terraces overlooking the ocean. Facilities include a wide beach, pool, tennis courts, and shopping arcade. Expensive. 1500 Orange Avenue, Coronado, CA 92118. 619/435-6611.

❂ *Hyatt Islandia.* Great views of the ocean and bay make this 423-room hotel a lovely retreat. The rooms are spacious, and facilities include a pool. Expensive. 1441 Quivira Road, San Diego, CA 92109. 619/224-1234.

❂ *Julian Hotel.* This historic 1897 Gold Rush Victorian offers 18 rooms, only 5 with private baths. The inn is in Julian, the mountain village that retains many touches from its gold boom days. Moderate. P.O. Box 1856, Julian, CA 92036. 619/765-0201.

❂ *Le Meridien.* Elegant and new, the finest rooms in this modern hotel face the water and the San Diego skyline. There are 300 rooms, all with French country decor. Facilities include a pool and spa. Expensive. 2000 Second Street, Coronado, CA 92118. 619/435-3000.

❂ *Monet's Garden.* There are four spacious suites in this beautiful inn. All the suites are furnished with antiques. The inn is surrounded by gardens and sculptures. Moderate. 7039 Casa Lane, San Diego, CA 91945. 619/464-8296.

❂ *Pinecroft Manor.* Two lovely rooms in this Tudor sheltered by pines near the gold-mining boomtown of Julian. The rooms are furnished with antiques. The rooms share a bath. Inexpensive. P.O. Box 655, Julian, CA 92036. 619/765-1611.

❂ *Rancho Valencia Resort.* Small and luxurious, this tennis resort in the hills north of San Diego has 43 beautiful suites located in 41 casitas, 18 tennis courts, a pool, spa, and other activities. Expensive. 5921 Valencia Circle, P.O. Box 9126, Rancho Santa Fe, CA 92067. 619/756-1123 and 800/548-3664 nationwide.

❂ *Sheraton Grand on Harbor Island.* The 350 rooms in this luxury hotel have rooms with views of the water and the many marinas in the area. Expensive. 1590 Harbor Island Drive, San Diego, CA 92101. 619/291-6400.

❂ *Westgate Hotel.* This 223-room high-rise overlooks the harbor and offers elegant accommodations and every possible service. Expensive. 1055 Second Avenue, San Diego, CA 92101. 619/238-1818.

San Diego: Fine Dining

❂ *The Abbey.* Excellent and consistent American regional cuisine. Moderate. 2825 Fifth Avenue. 619/291-4779.

❂ *Baci Ristorante.* Superb Northern Italian cuisine, with seafood the specialty. Moderate. 1955 West Molena Boulevard. 619/275-2094.

✪ *Belgian Lion.* Great roast duck and mixed service make this a wonderful but sometimes trying French restaurant. Expensive. 2265 Bacon Street. 619/223-2700.

✪ *Chez Loma.* This intimate restaurant serves excellent continental dishes. Moderate. 1132 Loma Avenue, Coronado. 619/435-0661.

✪ *Crown-Coronet Room.* Outstanding continental cuisine served in a large dining room decorated with a carved wooden ceiling and other touches worthy of a duke's hunting lodge. Expensive. Hotel del Coronado, 1500 Orange Avenue. 619/435-6611.

✪ *Dobson's.* Creative menu featuring seafood makes this stylish Californian-French restaurant a winner. Expensive. 956 Broadway Circle. 619/231-6771.

✪ *L'Escale.* Great views of the bay and the San Diego skyline make this fine Californian-French restaurant a romantic place. Expensive. Le Meridien, 2000 Second Street, Coronado. 619/435-3000.

✪ *Pacifica Grill.* Creative Southwestern cooking served in a remodeled warehouse. Moderate. 1202 Kettner Boulevard. 619/696-9226.

✪ *Panda Inn.* Sensational Chinese cuisine at this Horton Plaza restaurant. Inexpensive. 506 Horton Plaza. 619/233-7800.

(For more hotels, inns and restaurants, see the La Jolla section in Chapter One.)

San Francisco: Romantic Lodging

✪ *Alamo Square Inn.* Located in the historic district, this elegant 1895 Queen Anne has 13 beautifully furnished rooms, all but two of which have private baths. The inn also has a library, whirlpool, bicycles, and serene gardens. Moderate. 719 Scott Street, San Francisco, CA 94117. 415/922-2055 and 800/345-9888 nationwide.

✪ *Archbishops Mansion.* The 15 guest rooms in this beautifully restored 1904 belle epoque inn are named after nineteenth-century romantic operas and decorated in the theme. The opera connection, done lightly but nicely in the room decor, is inspired by the San Francisco Opera just 10 blocks away. Most of the rooms have fireplaces and great views of the city. Moderate/expensive. 1000 Fulton Street, San Francisco, CA 94117. 415/563-7872 and 800/543-5820 nationwide.

✪ *Art Center Bed and Breakfast.* French Colonial whose five rooms are furnished with antiques. The inn has lovely gardens, a library, and many fireplaces. Moderate. 1902 Filbert Street, San Francisco, CA 94123. 415/567-1526.

✪ *Chateau Tivoli.* Towers and turrets make this 1892 Victorian a picturesque inn. There are seven rooms, three with private baths. The furnishings are antique. Expensive. 1057 Steiner Street, San Francisco, CA 94115. 415/776-5462 and 800/228-1647 nationwide.

✪ *Edward II Inn.* Built for the 1915 Panama-Pacific Exposition, this magnificent Edwardian near Fisherman's Wharf has 29 rooms, 19 with private baths. The furnishings are English country. Expensive. 3155 Scott Street, San Francisco, CA 94123. 415/922-3000.

✪ *Fairmont Hotel and Tower.* The spectacular lobby is a nice buildup to the 596 spacious rooms in this stately hotel. Facilities include a health club. Expensive. 950 Mason Street, San Francisco, CA 94108. 415/772-5000 and 800/527-4727 nationwide.

✪ *Grand Hyatt.* Recently redecorated, this 693-room luxury hotel overlooks Union Square. Expensive. 345 Stockton Street, San Francisco, CA 94108. 415/398-1234 and 800/228-9000 nationwide.

✪ *Mark Hopkins.* This landmark hotel on Nob Hill offers 392 comfortable rooms redecorated recently in neoclassical furnishings. Ask for an even-numbered room; they have views of the Golden Gate Bridge. Expensive. 999 California Street, San Francisco, CA 94108. 415/392-3434 and 800/327-0200 nationwide.

✪ *Hotel Nikko–San Francisco.* Understated elegance makes this Japanese Air Lines hotel a fine retreat. The rooms are comfortable and very tastefully decorated. Expensive. 222 Mason Street, San Francisco, CA 94102. 415/394-1111 and 800/NIKKO-US nationwide.

✪ *Huntington Hotel.* Low-key but elegant, this Nob Hill hotel retains the finer touches of the great hotels of the past. The 140 rooms are tastefully decorated and comfortable. Expensive. 1075 California Street, San Francisco, CA 94108. 415/474-5400; and 800/652-1539 in California, 800/227-4683 elsewhere in the United States.

✪ *Hyatt Fisherman's Wharf.* Great location (on the wharf and next to the cable car line), great views of the city and the bay, superb accommodations make this new hotel an outstanding find. There are 313 rooms, all nicely decorated. Facilities include an exercise room and sauna. Expensive. 555 North Point Street, San Francisco, CA 94133. 415/563-1234.

✪ *Inn at the Opera.* Located next to the Civic Center's theaters, this hotel offers 48 lushly furnished rooms. It's a popular home away from home for the stars of the stages next door. Moderate/expensive. 333 Fulton Street, San Francisco, CA 94102. 415/863-8400 and 800/423-9610 nationwide.

❂ *Inn San Francisco.* This exquisite Italianate Victorian was built in 1872. Today it has 21 antique-filled rooms, 16 with private baths. The inn has hot tubs, a library, and a sundeck. Expensive. 943 South Van Ness Avenue, San Francisco, CA 94110. 415/641-0188 and 800/359-0913 nationwide.

❂ *Mansions Hotel.* This twin-turret Victorian has 29 rooms, all furnished with antiques. The inn has a whirlpool, library, and peaceful garden. Expensive. 2220 Sacramento Street, San Francisco, CA 94115. 415/929-9444 and 800/424-9444 nationwide.

❂ *Monte Cristo.* This former saloon and bordello is now a beautiful, antique-filled inn. There are 14 rooms, 11 with private baths. 600 Presidio Avenue, San Francisco, CA 94115. 415/931-1875.

❂ *Petite Auberge.* French country furnishings make this 26-room inn a very romantic retreat. Most of the rooms have fireplaces. Expensive. 863 Bush Street, San Francisco, CA 94108. 415/928-6000.

❂ *Regis.* Built in 1913 and renovated in 1987, this quiet, 86-room hotel offers beautiful rooms decorated with English and French antiques, canopy beds, and huge bathrooms. Moderate/ expensive. 490 Geary Street, San Francisco, CA 94102. 415/928-7900 and 800/827-3447 nationwide.

❂ *Ritz-Carlton.* This superluxury hotel, the newest on Nob Hill, offers 336 spacious and tastefully appointed rooms. Facilities include pool, whirlpool, and health club. Expensive. California at Stockton, San Francisco, CA 94108. 415/296-7465 and 800/ 241-3333 nationwide.

❂ *St. Francis.* Recently renovated, this grand hotel on Union Square remains a familiar and luxurious landmark. The 1,200 rooms range from nice but small to suites fit for a king. Expensive.

335 Powell Street, San Francisco, CA 94102. 415/397-7000 and 800/228-3000 nationwide.

✪ *Sherman House.* This renovated French-Italianate mansion was built in 1876 in the Pacific Heights neighborhood. Today it has 14 beautiful (and a bit overfurnished) rooms. The decor is French Empire with a sprinkling of other periods. Suites 302 and 401 each have a terrace and a view of the Golden Gate Bridge and Alcatraz. Expensive. 2160 Green Street, San Francisco, CA 94123. 415/563-3600.

✪ *Stanford Court.* Beautifully furnished, meticulous and thoughtful service, and located on Nob Hill. What more can you say about this 402-room hotel, one of the finest in the nation. Expensive. 905 California Street, San Francisco, CA 94108. 415/989-3500 and 800/227-4736 nationwide.

✪ *Victorian Inn on the Park.* Directly across from Golden Gate Park, this majestic Queen Anne–style Victorian has 12 rooms, each with a private bath. The inn has been beautifully restored. Moderate. 301 Lyon Street, San Francisco, CA 94117. 415/ 931-1830.

✪ *White Swan Inn.* This marble-faced inn near Union Square has 26 elegant rooms, all beautifully furnished with English antiques. The rooms have sitting areas and fireplaces. Expensive. 845 Bush Street, San Francisco, CA 94108. 415/775-5717.

San Francisco: Fine Dining

✪ *Acquerello.* Simple yet sumptuous Italian dishes make this romantic and cozy restaurant a find in Pacific Heights. Expensive. 1722 Sacramento Street. 415/567-5432.

✪ *Act IV, Inn at the Opera.* Strange name, but one that hides the fine Italian cooking and the intimate and romantic dining room. Expensive. 333 Fulton Street. 415/863-8400.

✪ *Amelio's.* Fine French cuisine that tastes as wonderful as it looks. Expensive. 1630 Powell Street. 415/397-4339.

✪ *L'Avenue.* Excellent American cuisine, a rare find in San Francisco. Moderate. 3854 Geary Boulevard. 415/386-1555.

✪ *Buca Giovanni.* Elegant Tuscany cooking in a romantic subterranean room. Moderate. 800 Greenwich Street. 415/776-7766.

✪ *Campton Place.* Superb American regional cuisine, with a hint of a Southern accent. Expensive. 340 Stockton Street. 415/781-5555.

✪ *Le Castel.* Creative French cuisine in a restaurant located in a Victorian house. Expensive. 3235 Sacramento Street. 415/921-7115.

✪ *Corona Bar and Grill.* Regional Mexican dishes, in a room mixing Old San Francisco and Old Mexico decor. Moderate. 88 Cyril Magnin. 415/392-5500.

✪ *Fleur de Lys.* This romantic dining room serves some of the finest French dishes in town. Expensive. 777 Sutton Street. 415/673-7779.

✪ *Fog City Diner.* You may know this diner from the credit card commercials. Thousands of other diners do, most attracted by the commercial and not the superb creative American regional cuisine. Moderate. 1300 Battery Street. 415/982-2000.

✪ *La Folie.* Small and colorful, this outstanding French restaurant may be the best in town. Expensive. 2316 Polk Street. 415/776-5577.

✪ *Hyde Street Bistro.* This small and intimate restaurant serves outstanding cuisine that is a marriage of Austrian and Italian. Moderate. 1521 Hyde Street. 415/441-7778.

✪ *Khan Toke Thai House.* The menu is extensive, and most of the dishes are excellent. Inexpensive. 5937 Geary Boulevard. 415/668-6654.

✪ *Mandarin.* Fantastic Chinese cuisine. Moderate. Ghiradelli Square. 415/673-8812.

✪ *New Asia.* Busy and yet entertaining, this superb restaurant serves outstanding dim sum. Inexpensive. 772 Pacific Avenue. 415/391-6666.

✪ *Ocean City.* Extensive dim sum menu and Szechuan and Cantonese cooking. Inexpensive. 640 Broadway. 415/982-2328.

✪ *1001 Nob Hill.* Exciting cuisine blending French, Pacific Rim, and American regional cuisine into something new and wonderful. The room is luxurious. Expensive. 1001 California Street. 415/441-1001.

✪ *Pacific Heights Bar and Grill.* The best oyster bar in town, as well as some of the best seafood. Moderate. 2001 Fillmore Street. 415/567-3337.

✪ *Postrio.* Yet another creation of Wolfgang Puck, this time mixing Californian, Italian, and Asian cuisines into an always surprising and wonderful combination. Expensive. 545 Post Street. 415/776-7825.

✪ *Splendido.* Excellent Mediterranean cuisine. Expensive. No. 4 Embarcadero. 415/986-3222.

✪ *Square One.* Mediterranean, Asian, and Latin dishes make this Embarcadero spot always a surprising restaurant. Expensive. 190 Pacific Avenue. 415/788-1110.

✪ *Stars.* Chef Jeremiah Tower claims to have invented Californian cuisine, and—true or not—his menu remains as inventive as ever. Expensive. 150 Redwood Alley. 415/861-7827.

✪ *Undici.* Splendid southern Italian and Sicilian dishes make this SoMa restaurant a winner. Moderate. 374 11th Street. 415/431-3337.

✪ *Wu Kong Shanghai Restaurant.* The weekend dim sum lunches are outstanding at this fine Shanghai restaurant. Moderate. One Rincon Center at 101 Spear Street. 415/957-9300.

✪ *Yamato.* This grand old Japanese restaurant is a beautiful room, decorated with fine woods, murals, and a garden. The sushi bar is great, better than the dishes on the limited menu. Moderate. 717 California Street. 415/397-3456.

✪ *Zuni Cafe Grill.* The Italian-Mediterranean cuisine is fine, but don't overlook the great pizzas and outstanding burgers. Moderate. 1658 Market Street. 415/552-2522.

✪ NIGHTLIFE

All three cities have many nightclubs, theaters, and symphony halls. A sampler of the best follows.

Los Angeles

The top stages are the Ahmanson Theater (135 North Grand Avenue, 213/972-7654), Mark Taper Forum (135 North Grand Avenue, 213/972-7353), Pantages (6233 Hollywood Boulevard, Hollywood, 213/410-1062), and the Wilshire Theater (8440 Wilshire Boulevard, 213/642-4242).

For classical music, the Ambassador Auditorium (300 West Green Street, Pasadena, 818/304-6161), Dorothy Chandler Pavilion (135 North Grand Avenue, 213/972-7211), the Hollywood Bowl (2301 Highland Avenue, 213/850-2000), and Royce Hall (405 North Hilgard Avenue, 213/825-9261) are the top forums in the city. Call for the schedule of events.

For jazz, visit the Baked Potato (3787 Cahuenga Boulevard West, North Hollywood, 818/980-1615) or the Vine Street Bar and Grill (1610 Vine Street, Hollywood, 213/463-4375). For rock, the in spot is always changing, but try McCabe's Guitar Shop (3101 Pico Boulevard, Santa Monica, 213/828-4497) and the Strand (1700 South Pacific Coast Highway, Redondo Beach, 213/316-1700).

La Cage aux Folles (643 North La Cienega Boulevard, West Hollywood, 213/657-1091) is a supper club with a sensational act by female impersonators. And for comedy, visit the Comedy and Magic Club (1018 Hermosa Avenue, Hermosa Beach, 213/372-2626), the Comedy Store (8433 Sunset Boulevard, Hollywood, 213/656-6225), or Second City (214 Santa Monica Boulevard, Santa Monica, 213/451-0621).

San Diego

The Bowery Theatre (1057 First Avenue, 619/232-4088), Old Globe Theatre (Simon Edison Centre, Balboa Park, 619/239-2255), and the Lyceum Theatre (Horton Plaza, 619/235-8025) are the top stages in town, offering dramas, comedies, and musicals year-round.

For classical music, Sherwood Auditorium (700 Prospect Street in La Jolla, 619/459-0267) draws internationally known ensembles, while the San Diego Symphony plays in Symphony Hall (1245 Seventh Avenue, 619/699-4205).

The San Diego Opera holds its four-opera season from January through April at Civic Theatre (202 C Street, 619/236-6510), and the California Ballet presents four productions from September through May at the same location. Call 619/560-5676 for ballet information.

The top jazz clubs are the B Street Cafe and Bar (425 West B Street, 619/236-1707) and Humphrey's (2241 Shelter Island Drive, 619/224-3577). For rock, try the funky Belly Up Tavern (143 South Cedros Avenue, Solana Beach, 619/481-9022).

The best piano bar is in the Westgate Hotel (1055 Second Avenue, 619/238-1818).

San Francisco

The top stages are the Curran (445 Geary Street, 415/673-4400), the Golden Gate (Golden Gate Avenue at Taylor Street, 415/474-3800), and the Orpheum (1192 Market Street, 415/ 474-3800). The top theater company in town is the American Conservatory Theatre (ACT), whose productions are at the Geary Theater (415 Geary Street, 415/749-2228).

For classical music, the Davis Symphony Hall (Van Ness Avenue at Grove Street) is home for the San Francisco Symphony. Call 415/431-5400 for the concert schedule. The San Francisco Ballet dances at the War Memorial Opera House (Van Ness Avenue at Grove Street, 415/621-3838). The San Francisco Opera sings at the opera house, too. Call 415/864-3330.

The top jazz club is Kimball's (300 Grove Street, 415/861-5555). For dance music, visit the New Orleans Room in the Fairmont Hotel (950 Mason Street, 415/772-5259).

The Great American Music Hall (859 O'Farrell Street, 415/885-0750) books top pop and rock stars. Just for laughs, stop in at Cobb's Comedy Club (The Cannery, 2801 Leavenworth, 415/928-4320), the Improv (401 Mason Street, 415/441-7787), and the Punchline (444-A Battery Street, 415/397-7573).

Chapter Seven

The Magnificent Mountains

The origin of California's rise to the status of superstate took place more than a century before the rise of Silicon Valley and a lifetime before Hollywood became a household name. California's future as a major world economic power was sealed in January 1848, when a millworker named Henry W. Bilger scrawled in his diary this fateful sentence: "Monday 24th this day some kind of mettle was found in the tail race that looks like goald first discovered by James Martial, the boss of the mill."

The sentence, misspellings and all, recorded the event—the discovery of gold at Sutter's Mill—that dramatically changed the state, the nation, and the world. The discovery set off the largest migration in history, attracting fortune seekers from around the world.

The prospectors—they were nicknamed the '49ers—were part of a crusade unlike anything ever seen before in this young nation.

A madness—Gold Fever—seized the countless thousands trying to scratch a fortune out of the earth. Some, a precious few, actually got wealthy from finding gold. Far more got rich by selling food, liquor, lodging, and other supplies to the dreamers.

The mountains maintain their hold on us. Where once gold lured thousands from around the world, now fantastic scenery and unspoiled wilderness draw millions of visitors each year. The names—Yosemite, Sequoia, Kings Canyon, and Lake Tahoe—are just as spellbinding as Angels Camp and Sutter Creek, the heart and soul of Gold Country. Go now and you will find that these mountains are still filled with riches.

✪ GOLD RUSH COUNTRY

The Gold Country is west of Sacramento, stretching approximately 200 miles along Highway 49 from Nevada City on the north to Sonora on the south. Once this region was the center of world attention. In its day, Nevada City was bigger and richer than San Francisco. Then the gold fever cooled, dreams faded, and the rush dwindled and died.

The Gold Country is a terrific weekend getaway. What you see are historic sites, antique shops, wineries, and quaint and colorful towns, all located in the scenic Sierra Nevada foothills.

Start a tour of the region in Nevada City, where the finds today are in the town's many antique shops. The Miners Foundry, built in 1865, holds the American Victorian Museum, which displays many Victorian artifacts and serves as the local cultural center. Next to the Foundry is the Nevada City Winery, located in the foundry's garage.

After browsing through Nevada City, head south on Highway 49 through Grass Valley, a mining town destroyed by fire in 1855 and then rebuilt. You can get a glimpse into mining life by stopping at the Empire Mine, which was once the state's biggest

✪ Emerald Bay, on Lake Tahoe. (Courtesy of Lake Tahoe Visitors Authority)

and richest gold mine, and the North Star Power House, both on Empire Street off Highway 49. The Empire Mine produced gold from 1850 to 1956. It's now a state park and tours are conducted through the mining buildings and tunnels. The North Star Power House, a forerunner of today's hydroelectric generators, powered the mining operations. Exhibits include old mining buildings, mining equipment, and hands-on exhibits.

The names of the mining towns along Highway 20 west of Grass Valley say a lot about the character of the era: Rough and Ready (which seceded from the Union in 1850 and returned, a bit belatedly, in 1948), Timbuctoo, Smartville, and French Corral.

The next stop on Highway 49 is Auburn, a quaint and colorful town with cobblestone roads and wooden sidewalks. Its Bernhard Museum exhibits artifacts from the late Victorian era.

South of Auburn is Coloma, where it all started at John Sutter's famous mill. The Marshall Gold Discovery State Historic Park, which encompasses much of the town, has a replica of Sutter's Mill, a museum, and picnic areas.

Ten miles farther south is Placertown, where you can tour two gold mines at the Gold Bug Park. The next interesting town on Highway 49 is Sutter Creek, a well-preserved mining town which now boasts numerous antique and art shops. South of Sutter Creek, the highway begins to twist as it climbs into the mountains to towns like Jackson, Mokelumne Hill, and Angels Camp. The latter was made famous when Bret Harte featured it in his yarn *Luck of Roaring Camp* and Mark Twain wrote about its jumping frog contest in his story *The Jumping Frog of Calaveras County.* The contest is part of a festival held every May.

Ten miles east of Angels Camp on Highway 4 is Murphys, a lively town with many interesting Victorian homes. Murphys and its gold mining operations attracted such visiting personages as Ulysses S. Grant, J. Pierpont Morgan, and Horatio Alger. Main Street is the place for antique shops, restaurants, and the theater with the latest production by "The Black Bart Players."

The courthouse is also the museum, where the exhibits include an old cell with the writing *Black Bart Slept Here.* Black Bart, an infamous stagecoach robber, was jailed and tried in the building.

Murphys also has three interesting wineries. The Black Sheep Vintners, in an old barn at the west end of Main Street, offers tours on weekends. The Millier Winery, on School Street a block north of Highway 4, is a tiny operation located in the basement of the Milliers' home, and the Stevenot is located in a gorge on San Domingo Road.

Four miles farther east on Highway 4 is the Moaning Cavern, a huge cave with odd and beautiful rock formations. You can tour 800 feet of galleries in the caverns, which are named for the sound that used to come out of its mouth. The moan disappeared when a staircase was built into the cave.

Fifteen miles farther is the Calaveras Big Trees State Park, where the towering sequoias live. Hike the nature trail and you come to a staircase that leads to an incredible 24-foot-wide stump of a sequoia.

Return to Highway 49 and drive south through the rugged countryside for about 12 miles to the turnoff for Columbia State Historic Park, a restored gold mining town that offers stagecoach rides, a place to pan for gold, a playhouse, and other diversions.

The last stop on this tour of Gold Country is Sonora, whose mixed heritage is evident in its elegant Victorian homes and numerous adobes. Photographs and other exhibits from the Gold Rush Era can be seen in the Tuolumne County Museum.

One other city in Gold Rush Country is worth a sidetrip or a return visit to explore its wonders. Sacramento, the state capital, is the site of one of the largest restored districts of nineteenth-century buildings in the nation.

Old Sacramento is bounded by the Sacramento River and Interstate 5, between L and H streets. The visitors center is a former train depot, and the Sacramento History Center was once the city hall. The California State Railroad Museum displays 21 working locomotives and cars while other restored buildings hold shops and restaurants.

Outside Old Sacramento are other attractions. The Crocker Art Museum is the oldest in the west and known for its collection of European and Asian art. The Towe Ford Museum has a copy of every model made by Ford over a half century. And Sutter's Fort, the original settlement created by John Augustus Sutter in 1839, displays artifacts from the period.

✪ LAKE TAHOE

Spectacular is the only word to describe this emerald-green 482-square-mile lake that straddles the California-Nevada border in the Sierra Nevada.

The lake, located at more than 6,000 feet above sea level, offers a world of getaway possibilities. In the winter, the Tahoe region is a popular winter sports resort. The temperatures are fairly mild, considering the elevation: an average high of 36 degrees and a low of 18 degrees. When the snows go, boaters, hikers, campers, and—yes—gamblers come to enjoy the beautiful lake and the national forests that surround it.

The lake is a wonderful escape from the sizzling heat of California's central valleys and southern cities. Daytime highs in July and August are in the 70s, with nightly lows in the 40s.

The region's unparalleled beauty has drawn visitors for generations. There are 19 major ski resorts, 23 campgrounds, and hundreds of other inns and hotels in the region.

The most scenic route to Lake Tahoe is Interstate 80 to Highway 89 south. The interstate approaches from the north, passing through Gold Country, the Donner Pass, and Tahoe National Forest. The scenery along this route is sensational.

Highway 89 passes through Squaw Valley and reaches the lake at Tahoe City, where the best exhibits on the area's history are at the Gatekeepers Log Cabin Museum.

The drive around the lake is wonderful. The rugged western shore offers some spectacular views of the lake, which always seems to be in sight, while the less-mountainous southern and eastern shores are more built up. You can drive completely around the lake by taking the shore road, which changes numbers along the way. Taking the 72-mile drive is possible in a day. Take a picnic along and stop for lunch at a roadside park where the views are often quite stunning.

From Tahoe City, drive south on Highway 89 to the Sugar Pine State Park, a pleasant park whose main attraction is the Ehrman Mansion, a 1903 stone summer home that's open for tours.

Farther south is first the D. L. Bliss State Park, a popular camping spot, and then Emerald Bay, easily the most beautiful part of the lake. From your high vantage point, the deep waters look emerald green. The lake averages 989 feet in depth and the water is so clear that divers can see more than 200 feet. The bay, a chubby finger of water, surrounds Lake Tahoe's only island, Fannette.

From the Inspiration Point lookout, hike the 1-mile trail to Vikingsholm, a 38-room mansion inspired by a 1,200-year-old Viking fortress. The rough stone mansion is open for tours. Before you go be prepared for the hike. The trail is rugged, and returning is more difficult than going to Vikingsholm.

West of Emerald Bay is the Desolation Wilderness, a 63,000-acre preserve whose glacier-polished fields of stone are almost completely bare of trees. Elevations within the wilderness range from 6,500 to 10,000 feet. There are more than 50 miles of trails linking the many lakes and streams in the region. If you are interested in hiking into the region, stop at the Forest Service Visitors Center in South Lake Tahoe for maps and other information.

The visitors center is south of Emerald Bay on Highway 89. The center's staff has more information on the lake and adjacent parklands and exhibits on the region's ecosystem.

Past the center, Highway 89 meets U.S. 50, which you will follow around the lake to South Lake Tahoe and, a few miles farther, Stateline, the aptly named town that is in both Califor-

Winter Wonderlands

Lake Tahoe is famous for its fine ski resorts. Among the top resorts is Squaw Valley, site of the 1960 Olympic winter games. The valley doesn't have runs; it has snow fields— more than 8,300 acres of fields, which have slopes for every skill level. For accommodations, call 916/583-6985 or 800/545-4350 nationwide.

Alpine Meadows has the longest ski season, from Thanksgiving through May, thanks to its base elevation of 6,835 feet. The resort has 2,000 acres of ski terrain. Call 916/525-5273 for Rockwood Lodge, an upscale bed-and-breakfast, or the Tahoe Vista Inn and Marina, a luxurious lake hideaway, at 916/546-4819.

Northstar-at-Tahoe is a complete resort with 1,700 acres of tree-lined runs and every facility and package skiers need. Call 916/562-1010 and 800/533-6787 nationwide.

Heavenly Valley is the largest ski resort in the nation. It has 12,800 acres of ski terrain, a 5.5-mile run, vertical face of 3,600 feet, and the highest elevation (10,100 feet). Call the Eagle's Nest, 702/588-6492, which is a luxurious inn, or the Ridge Tahoe, 800/648-3391 nationwide, an inn with private gondolas to the Heavenly Valley slopes.

Kirkwood isn't as flashy as Heavenly Valley, but it remains a fine ski resort with 2,000 acres of ski terrain, a base of 7,800 feet (the highest in the state), and great facilities. Sun Meadow, a nice condo unit, is the preferred accommodation. Call 209/258-6000.

The Tahoe Nordic Ski Center has 67 kilometers of trails, a vertical drop of 1,000 feet, 2,000 acres of ski terrain, and an excellent ski school. Call 916/583-9858.

nia and Nevada. This is the commercial region of the lakeshore. Here you will find the big casinos, the major resorts, the glitter and the flash of Las Vegas–style entertainment.

U.S. 50 passes through this neon jungle and continues north along the lakeshore through small recreation areas and lesser marvels of nature until it meets Highway 28. Take this road along the north shore until you return to Highway 89. The most popular sight along this stretch of highway isn't the roulette wheels in Crystal Bay's casinos. It's the Ponderosa Ranch, east of Incline Village just off Highway 28. The long-running television series "Bonanza" was filmed here. Attractions include a western town, saloon, hayrides, and the Cartwrights' ranch house.

✪ SEQUOIA AND KINGS CANYON NATIONAL PARKS

This superpark—36 miles wide and 66 miles long—features enormous trees, an immense canyon, and the tallest mountain—Mt. Whitney (14,495 feet)—in the continental states.

You enter these parks via Highway 198 from Visalia or Highway 180 from Fresno. There are more attractions than can be seen in a day or a week, but the major sights are the sequoias in the Giant Forest, Grant Grove, and along Generals Highway and the beautiful Cedar Grove Valley of Kings Canyon.

From the Ash Mountain Entrance (Highway 198), you can take a 48-mile drive through the giant trees that give their name to Sequoia National Park. Drive first to the Hospital Rock, 6 miles into the park, where you can see exhibits about the Indians who once lived here. Eleven miles farther is the Giant Forest, where you can see the world's largest living tree, named many years ago for General Sherman. The tree is 274 feet tall, 102 feet around, and more than 2,700 years old. From here drive north on the Generals Highway and drive northwest until you come to Highway 180 in the Sequoia National Forest. Turn north and continue to the Grant Grove Visitor Center (part of Kings Canyon, although separated from the main park). The left turn just beyond the center leads to trails that you can hike to more giant trees and one named after a Union general—Ulysses S. Grant. The General Grant is 267 feet tall and 107 feet around.

The last stop on this trip is Panoramic Point, reached by taking the steep 2.5-mile road east of the visitor center. From this lookout you can see the Sierra Nevada range.

The next suggested trip is 36 miles long and goes to Cedar Grove, a mile-deep valley with rushing streams and thick stands of pine, fir, and oak. To reach it, drive north and east on Highway 180 from Grants Grove until the road ends. Numerous hiking trails lead into the valley from the Cedar Grove Village (you pass it going in). These trails give you a closer look at the waterfalls and other delights of this unspoiled valley paradise.

Another favorite attraction in this landscape cannot be seen from the air. It's underground. The Crystal Cave is a stunning marble cavern. You can visit it in the summer by taking the Generals Highway south from Giant Forest Village to the unpaved road. Turn right and drive 9 miles (it may take an hour) to the cave parking area. Guided tours are offered from 10 AM to 3 PM each day.

Mt. Whitney straddles the border of Sequoia National Park and the Inyo National Forest. You can hike into its lower elevations from the Crabtree ranger station. Ask for a map at the visitor center.

As in Yosemite, the park rangers conduct a full range of activities, from hikes and photography expeditions to nature classes and evening singalongs. The park newspaper available in the visitor center will list the full schedule.

✪ YOSEMITE NATIONAL PARK

"No temple made with hands," wrote naturalist John Muir, "can compare with Yosemite."

Roughly the size of Rhode Island (761,757 acres), this marvelous wonderland is reached by taking Highway 140 from the west, Highway 41 from the south, or Highway 120 from the northeast or the west.

The park attracts more than 3 million visitors a year, almost all of whom go to 1 percent of the park's area: the Yosemite Valley, a 1-mile-wide and 7-mile-long canyon carved by a river. Flanked by majestic mountains, this valley is a stunning work of nature, and it is just a small part of the fantastic scenery in the park. There is so much to see that we offer a short list of the top attractions. These are the Yosemite Valley, the sequoias of Mariposa Grove, the views from Glacier Point, and the alpine country found on the Tioga Road.

You can drive through the valley, but the roads are one-way and often crowded with traffic in summer. A more pleasant way to tour the valley is by taking the free shuttle bus. Outside the valley, you can drive, bike, or hike to the other attractions on your own.

You catch the free shuttle bus at the parking lots at the east end of the valley. The first stop is the Yosemite Village and the Valley Visitor Center, which offers exhibits, brochures, maps, and a slide show on the park. You can take a short hike along a marked trail from the center to Cook's Meadow, or walk over to the Indian Village and the Indian Cultural Center. Indians lived in the valley centuries before the first European ever saw the landscape, and exhibits and bark house in the village explore their history. The center displays art created by area tribes.

The next stop on the bus route is Yosemite Falls, whose upper and lower sections form the highest cascade (2,425 feet) in North America and the second highest in the world. The lower section is a one-quarter-mile walk from the bus stop, the upper falls a difficult 3.5-mile hike. The views from the upper falls are spectacular, but the hike—a difficult climb rising 2,650 feet—is an all-day event for experienced hikers.

The next stunning sight is El Capitan, whose 3,000-foot wall of stone is a familiar scene for photographers and artists. Rock climbers often can be seen on the wall. The giant granite masses of Sentinel Rock and Glacier Point loom nearby as the bus heads to the Happy Isles Nature Center, which is on two river islands linked by a bridge. On the northeast horizon is Half Dome, which soars almost a mile above the valley as it reaches 8,842 feet in height.

The route to Glacier Point and Mariposa Grove is Highway 41 (the Wawona Road). This drive is 52 miles long and leaves the valley through the Wawona Tunnel. Stop at the parking area at the east end of the tunnel and look back at some of the most magnificent scenery on the planet. Half Dome, Sentinel Rock, El Capitan, and the 620-foot Bridal Veil waterfall can be seen from this point. The vista is simply incredible.

When you can tear yourself away from this vista, continue through the tunnel, and drive to the Glacier Point Road and turn left. The 16-mile road ends in a parking area and lookout giving yet another fantastic view of the valley and mountains.

Return to Highway 41 and drive south to Wawona and the Pioneer Yosemite History Center. In the summer, costumed actors re-create nineteenth-century life in this town.

The next stop, the sequoias of the Mariposa Grove, is located on a turnoff just beyond the south entrance to the park. Guided tours of these towering trees are offered from May through October. The oldest living tree is the Grizzly Giant, more than 27 centuries old.

Another tour out of the valley takes you onto Tioga Road to the alpine country. Take Highway 120 west for 9 miles to Crane Flat and turn right on the Tioga Road. It's a steep climb, but this 124-mile roundtrip drive carries you past mountain meadows, unspoiled lakes, and snow-covered summits usually unseen by most park visitors.

There are frequent turnoffs, for the scenery along the way is memorable. Forty miles from the valley is the Tuolumne Meadows Visitor Center. In the spring and summer, millions of wildflowers cover the meadow. Marsh marigolds, Lewis paintbrushes, and other colorful blossoms give the meadow the feel of a colorful impressionist landscape.

Hiking trails covering a wide range of length and difficulty lead out from the visitor center, the place to stop for gas, maps, and other information about this area of the park.

Beyond the center, the road continues to climb, finally reaching the Tioga Pass, at 9,945 feet the highest pass in California. Hiking trails from this pass lead to Upper Gaylor Lake and the ruins of a silver-mining camp.

These wonderful attractions are just the major points of a park that is open year-round. The best time to visit is not the summer, although it may be the best time for you. The summer is when the crowds come, jamming the valley roads, crowding the shops, and generally cluttering the scenery.

During the spring and fall, particularly during midweek, the park is uncrowded and wonderful. The park is beautiful even in winter, though bad weather closes many of the mountain roads and the Highway 120 entrance on the north side.

There is more to do than just gaze in awe at the stunning scenery. Park rangers conduct walks, hikes, photography expeditions, and other programs every day. These are listed in *The Yosemite Guide,* the free newspaper given away at the visitor center.

Whenever you go, take time to enjoy the romantic views with the person you are with. There is nothing to compare anywhere else in the world.

✪ FOR MORE INFORMATION

Gold Rush Country

Golden Chain Council of the Mother Lode. 685 Placerville Drive, Suite 412-49, Placerville, CA 95667.

Sacramento Convention and Visitors Bureau. 1421 K Street, Sacramento, CA 95814. 916/442-5542.

Lake Tahoe

Lake Tahoe Visitors Authority. 1156 Ski Run Boulevard, P.O. Box 16299, South Lake Tahoe, CA 95706. 916/544-5050 and 800/822-5922 nationwide.

Desolation Wilderness. 870 Emerald Bay Road, Box 731002, South Lake Tahoe, CA 95731. 916/573-2600.

Sequoia and Kings Canyon National Parks

Sequoia and Kings Canyon National Parks. Three Rivers, CA 93271. 209/565-3456.

Yosemite National Park

National Park Service Information Office. Box 577, Yosemite National Park, CA 95389. 209/372-0265.

✪ WHERE AND WHEN

Gold Rush Country

Bernhard Museum. 291 Auburn-Folsom Road, Auburn. Open 10 AM to 4 PM Tuesday through Sunday. 916/885-0264.

Black Sheep Vintners. Murphys Grade Road and Main Street, Murphys. Tours 12 AM to 5 PM Saturday and Sunday. 209/728-2157.

Calaveras Big Trees State Park. On Highway 4, 25 miles east of Murphys. Open daily. 209/795-2334.

California State Railroad Museum. 111 I Street, Sacramento. Open 10 AM to 5 PM daily. 916/448-4466.

Columbia State Historical Park. Off Highway 49 between Sonora and Murphys. Open daily. 209/532-4301.

Crocker Art Museum. 216 O Street, Sacramento. Open 1 PM to 9 PM Tuesday, 10 AM to 5 PM Wednesday through Sunday. 916/449-5423.

Empire Mine State Historical Park. 10791 East Empire Street, Grass Valley. Open daily. 916/273-8522.

Gold Bug Park. Off Bedford exit north from Highway 49 in Placerville. Park open 8 AM to sunset daily. Mine open April through October. 916/622-0832.

Marshall Gold Discovery State Historic Park. 310 Back Street, Coloma. Open 10 AM to 5 PM daily. 916/622-3470.

Millier Winery. 99 School Street, Murphys. Tours by appointment. 209/728-1100.

Miners Foundry. 325 Spring Street, Nevada City. Call for information about hours. 916/265-2692.

Moaning Cavern. On Vallecito-Columbia Highway 4 miles east of Murphys. Open 9 AM to 6 PM daily in summer, 10 AM to 5 PM daily in winter. 209/736-2708.

Nevada City Winery. 321 Spring Street, Nevada City. Tours noon to 5 PM daily. 916/265-9463.

North Star Power House. Allison Ranch Road and Mill Street in Grass Valley. Open 10 AM to 5 PM daily May through October. 916/273-4255.

Old Sacramento. Bounded by Front and Third streets between the Capitol Mall and J Street. Open daily. 916/442-5542.

Stevenot Winery. 2690 San Domingo Road, Murphys. Open 10 AM to 5 PM daily. 209/728-3436.

Sutter's Fort. 2701 L Street, Sacramento. Open 10 AM to 5 PM daily. 916/445-4422.

Towe Ford Museum. 2200 Front Street, Sacramento. Open 10 AM to 6 PM daily. 916/442-6802.

Tuolumne County Museum. 158 West Bradford Avenue, Sonora. Open 9 AM to 4:30 PM Monday, Wednesday, and Friday, 10 AM to 3:30 PM the rest of the week; closed on Sundays in the summer. 209/532-1317.

Lake Tahoe

Ehrman Mansion. Sugar Pine Point State Park, Highway 89. Open 11 AM to 4 PM daily July through September. 916/525-7232.

Gatekeeper's Log Cabin Museum. 139 West Lake Boulevard, Tahoe City. Open 11 AM to 5 PM daily May 15 through October 15. 916/583-1762.

Ponderosa Ranch. Highway 28, east of Incline Village. Open 9:30 AM to 6 PM daily April through October. 702/831-0691.

Vikingsholm. Emerald Bay, Highway 89. Open 10 AM to 4 PM daily June through September. 916/525-7277.

❂ ROMANTIC RETREATS

Here are our favorite romantic retreats, but first an explanation of how we break down our cost categories:

One night in a hotel, resort, or inn for two:

Inexpensive	Less than $50
Moderate	$50 to $100
Expensive	More than $100

Dinner for two (drinks not included):

Inexpensive	Less than $25
Moderate	$25 to $60
Expensive	More than $60

Gold Country, by City: Romantic Lodging and Fine Dining

Amador: Romantic Lodging

❂ *Mine House Inn.* This restored headquarters of the century-old Keystone Consolidated Mining Co. has seven lovely rooms, all furnished with Victorian antiques. Facilities include a pool. Moderate. Box 226, Highway 49, Amador, CA 95601. 209/267-5900.

Amador: Fine Dining

❂ *Au Relais.* Fine French cuisine in an elegant dining room adorned with crystal, fresh flowers, and rose linens make this an exceptional find. Moderate. 14220 Highway 49. 209/267-5636.

Auburn: Romantic Lodging

❂ *Victorian Hill House.* Antiques fill the four guest rooms and gardens surround the romantic 1884 Victorian on a hill overlooking the town. Facilities include a pool and hot tub. Moderate. P.O. Box 9097, Auburn, CA 95604. 916/885-5879.

Auburn: Fine Dining

❂ *Butterworth's.* Huge servings of American regional cuisine in a Victorian on a hill overlooking the town. Moderate. 1522 Lincoln Way. 916/885-0249.

❂ *Cafe Delicias.* Excellent Mexican food and enormous portions at this dining room in the historic area of Auburn. Inexpensive. 1591 Lincoln Way. 916/885-3598.

❂ *Headquarter House.* Great views from this hilltop dining room, with excellent Californian cuisine and fresh seafood. Moderate. 14500 Musso Road. 916/878-1906.

Coloma: Romantic Lodging

❂ *Coloma Country Inn.* This Victorian inn was built in 1852 and restored to its full magnificence. There are five rooms, three with private baths. It's furnished with interesting antiques. Expensive. Box 502, 2 High Street, Coloma, CA 95613. 916/622-6919.

❂ *Vineyard House.* Located on the site of a former winery, this lovely 1878 inn offers flower gardens and seven rooms furnished with period antiques. All the rooms share baths. Moderate. Box 176, Cold Springs Road, Coloma, CA 95613. 916/622-2217.

Coloma: Fine Dining

❂ *Vineyard House.* American regional cuisine served in a restored inn. Moderate. Cold Springs Road. 916/622-2217.

Grass Valley: Romantic Lodging

❂ *Murphy's Inn.* Once the home of a gold baron, this magnificent Greek Revival offers eight lovely guest rooms, all furnished with antique pieces. Six of the rooms have private baths. For a very private and romantic getaway, stay in the Donation Day House, where French doors separate the sitting area from the bedroom. There's a wood-burning stove opposite and a white iron bed. Moderate. 318 Neal Street, Grass Valley, CA 95945. 916/273-6873.

Grass Valley: Fine Dining

❂ *Owl Tavern.* Mouthwatering steaks, selected by you from a case and then grilled to order, are the stars at this cozy spot. The seafood dishes are also excellent. Moderate. 134 Mill Road. 916/273-0526.

Murphys: Romantic Lodging

❂ *Dunbar House 1880.* This 1880 Italianate Victorian inn offers four rooms, antiques, and gardens. Expensive. 271 Jones Street, Murphys, CA 95247. 209/728-2897.

Murphys: Fine Dining

For fine dining, head to nearby Sonora or Jamestown.

❂ *Hemingway's Cafe.* The menu is a United Nations of entrees, featuring Spanish dishes as well as more familiar French and Italian main courses. Good wine list. Moderate. 362 South Stewart, Sonora. 209/532-4900.

❂ *Jamestown Hotel.* Victorian antiques and a menu of solid American regional entrees make this a find in gold country. Moderate. Main Street, Sonora. 209/984-3902.

Nevada City: Romantic Lodging

✪ *Downey House.* The inn is an elegant Victorian, and the decor is Southwestern in the six rooms. All the rooms have private baths and identical decor. Moderate. 517 West Broad Street, Nevada City, CA 95959. 916/265-2815.

✪ *Flume's End.* This charming 150-year-old house sits above a rushing mountain stream. There are two pleasant rooms in the house and a romantic honeymoon cottage for those seeking more privacy. Moderate. 317 South Pine Street, Nevada City, CA 95959. 916/265-9665.

✪ *Grandmere's Bed and Breakfast Inn.* Built in 1856 and re-stored in 1985, this huge white Victorian has six rooms, country French decor, and antique furnishings. Expensive. 449 Broad Street, Nevada City, CA 95959. 916/265-4660.

✪ *The Red Castle.* A stunning 1860 Gothic Revival, with red brick and white trim. There are six antique-filled rooms with private baths and two that share a bath. Expensive. 109 Prospect Street, Nevada City, CA 95959. 916/265-5135.

Nevada City: Fine Dining

✪ *Country Rose.* The building is from the Gold Rush days, the furnishings are antique, and the menu is country French, and very nice country French at that. Moderate. 300 Commercial Street. 916/265-6248.

Placerville: Romantic Lodging

✪ *Combellack-Blair House.* This elegant Victorian house offers two rooms with exquisite period furnishings. The rooms share a bath. Moderate. 3059 Cedar Ravine, Placerville, CA 95667. 916/622-3764.

Placerville: Fine Dining

✪ *Powell Brothers Steamer Co.* The shellfish is the king at this nautical-decor restaurant. Moderate. 425 Main Street. 916/626-1091.

Sacramento: Romantic Lodging

✪ *Briggs House Bed and Breakfast.* Seven spacious rooms tastefully furnished with period antiques make this majestic 1901 Victorian an exceptional inn. Expensive. 2209 Capitol Avenue, Sacramento, CA 95816. 916/441-3214.

✪ *Hotel el Rancho Resort.* Created with recreation in mind, this 254-room resort offers tennis courts, racquetball, a fitness center, and exercise equipment. The rooms are comfortable and nicely furnished. Moderate. 1029 West Capitol Avenue, West Sacramento, CA 95691. 916/371-6731 and 800/952-5566 in California.

✪ *Sterling Hotel.* This inn is small (only 12 rooms) but it is a wonderful, romantic getaway. It has a concierge, an unusual glass structure used for private meetings, and lovely rooms with whirlpools and balconies. Some rooms have fireplaces. Expensive. 1300 H Street, Sacramento, CA 95814. 916/448-1300 and 800/365-7660 nationwide.

Sacramento: Fine Dining

✪ *Biba.* Popular with Californian politicians, this modern restaurant serves exceptional veal dishes, accompanied by a pianist. Expensive. 2801 Capitol Avenue. 916/445-2422.

✪ *Chantrelle.* This fine restaurant is located in the elegant Sterling Hotel and offers an exceptional French menu. Expensive. 1300 H Street. 916/442-0451.

✿ *The Firehouse.* Superb continental cuisine served in a very formal setting. Expensive. 1112 2nd Street. 916/442-4772.

Sutter Creek: Romantic Lodging

✿ *The Foxes Bed and Breakfast.* The name alone would be enough to love this inn. The six rooms are beautifully furnished with antiques in this restored 1857 house. Three rooms have fireplaces. Expensive. Box 159, 77 Main Street, Sutter Creek, CA 95685. 209/267-5882.

✿ *Hanford House.* The eight rooms in this former warehouse are spacious and beautifully furnished. All the rooms have private modern baths, high ceilings, and one (the Honeymoon Suite) has a fireplace. Moderate. 3 Hanford Street, P.O. Box 847, Sutter Creek, CA 95685. 209/267-0747.

✿ *Sutter Creek Inn Bed and Breakfast.* This 140-year-old New England–style house offers 19 rooms, each furnished with a wide mixture of antiques. Some beds are even hanging on chains from the ceiling. Expensive. Box 385, 75 Main Street, Sutter Creek, CA 95685. 209/267-5606.

Sutter Creek: Fine Dining

✿ *Pelargonium.* This art-filled cottage serves excellent Californian cuisine featuring seafood. Moderate. Highway 49 and Hanford Street. 209/267-5008.

Lake Tahoe: Romantic Lodging

✿ *Harrah's Tahoe Hotel/Casino.* There are 535 luxurious rooms in this 18-story highrise. Most rooms have two full baths (with telephones and TVs, of course), and many have stunning views of the lake. Facilities include a nightclub, casino, indoor pool, hot tubs, and health club. Expensive. Box 8, Stateline, NV 89449. 702/588-6606 and 800/648-3773 nationwide.

✪ *High Sierra Casino/Hotel.* French beaux arts meets the Old West in this renovated 537-room hotel. The rooms are spacious, and the decorator obviously loves mirrors. Facilities include a casino, pool, and hot tubs. Expensive. Box C, Stateline, NV 89449. 702/588-6211 and 800/322-7723 nationwide.

✪ *Hyatt Lake Tahoe Resort Hotel.* This luxury lakefront hotel offers 460 spacious rooms, a beach, pool, spa, tennis, health club, and a casino. Expensive. Lakeshore and Country Club Drive, Box 3239, Incline Village, NV 89450. 702/831-1111.

✪ *Mayfield House.* This cozy, 60-year-old cottage in the tall trees offers six comfortable rooms, all furnished with some nice Queen Anne pieces as well as more contemporary items. The rooms share baths. Moderate. 236 Grove Street, Tahoe City, CA 95730. 916/583-1001.

✪ *River Ranch.* The 22 comfortable, antique-filled rooms in this cozy lodge overlook the Truckee River. Moderate. Box 197, Tahoe City, CA 95730. 916/583-4264 and 800/535-9900 in California.

✪ *Sunnyside Lodge.* This modern lakeside lodge offers 23 spacious rooms, all nicely decorated with country pieces. Expensive. 1850 West Lake Boulevard, Tahoe City, CA 95730. 916/583-7200 and 800/822-2754 in California.

Lake Tahoe: Fine Dining

For fine dining, many of the top restaurants are in the lodges (River Ranch and the Sunnyside Inn—American menus and moderate prices—and the bigger hotel/casinos, which offer a wide array of choices and prices). Some other choices are:

✪ *La Petit Pier.* Romantic lakeside dining with fine French cuisine. Moderate. 7250 North Lake Boulevard, Tahoe Vista. 916/546-4464.

✪ *Wolfdale's.* Interesting and creative Californian-Japanese cuisine served in a beautiful lakefront room. Moderate. 640 North Lake Boulevard, Tahoe City. Moderate. 916/583-5700.

Yosemite National Park: Romantic Lodging

Lodging in Yosemite National Park is managed by the Yosemite Park & Curry Company. Call Central Reservations (5410 East Home, Fresno, CA 93727) at 209/252-4848. Choices for a romantic room include:

✪ *Ahwahnee Hotel.* Kings, emperors, stars, and presidents have stayed in this magnificent stone-and-log mountain lodge. It has 123 rooms, great views, and a waiting list. Expensive.

✪ *Yosemite Lodge.* Rustic motel rooms or even more rustic cabins, which come without baths. Great setting near Yosemite Falls. Facilities include a restaurant and pool. The lodge has 484 rooms. Moderate.

Yosemite National Park: Fine dining

✪ *Ahwahnee Hotel.* Very good steaks and fish served in an elegant mountain lodge. Expensive. Yosemite Village. 209/372-1489.

✪ *Erna's Elderberry House.* This small dining spot is located just outside the park, in Oakhurst. The menu is Californian-continental and the dishes are very good. Expensive. 48688 Victoria Lane, Oakhurst. 209/683-6800.

Sequoia and Kings Canyon Parks: Romantic Lodging

✿ *Giant Forest.* Rustic one- and two-bedroom cabins with baths. Some cabins come with wood-burning stoves. Inexpensive. Sequoia Guest Services, Box 789, Three Rivers, CA 93271. 209/561-3314.

Sequoia and Kings Canyon Parks: Fine Dining

Fine dining in these parks is a bit hard to come by. The best of a mediocre lot is the Giant Forest Lodge, which serves an American menu at moderate prices. The lodge is in the Giant Forest Village.

Chapter Eight

❖

Journeys into Adventure

Sometimes, the usual getaways aren't enough. No matter how elegant, how interesting, or how romantic a destination is, we need a getaway that exposes us to new challenges, new adventures, and new thrills.

California is an action-packed playground with rugged mountains, raging rivers, and scenic parks offering challenges and adventures year-round. On your next getaway, consider taking a raft ride on the white water of a raging river, or soaring high over the wine country in a hot-air balloon, or just sailing off the coast of sunny Southern California.

The potential seems endless for these Californian adventures. Here are some of our proposals. When you call, ask the outfitter whether any special equipment or clothing is required.

221

✪ BACKPACKING

✪ All-Outdoors Adventure Trips. Five-day backpacking trips in the high Sierras with time for photography, fishing, and other activities. The outfitter provides food, camping gear, and transportation. The cost is about $175 per person. 2151 San Miguel Drive, Walnut Creek, CA 94596. 415/932-8993.

✪ Shasta Llamas. Stephen Biggs specializes in hiking and camping trips where the heavy work—carrying the gear—is done by llamas. The trips in the northern California mountains usually involve about 5 to 10 miles of hiking a day. The trips cost about $80 to $100 per person a day and include food but not sleeping gear. They last from three to five days and are offered from June through September. P.O. Box 1137-AT, Mt. Shasta, CA 96067. 916/926-3959.

✪ BALLOONING

✪ Balloon Aviation of Napa Valley. Soar high over the vineyards at sunrise and then descend an hour later for a champagne reception. The cost is $125 per person. P.O. Box 3298, 2299 Third Street, Napa, CA 94558. 707/252-7067.

✪ A Balloon Tour by Pacific Horizons. Soar over the San Diego coastline, daily at sunrise and sunset. The costs vary according to the trip you desire. Call for more information. 16236 San Diequito Road, P.O. Box 8737, Ranch Santa Fe, CA 92067. 619/756-1790.

✪ A Beautiful Morning Balloon Co. Take a romantic flight over Del Mar with champagne and hors d'oeuvres. The costs vary, so

✪ Hot-air ballooning is a popular activity throughout California. (Palm Springs Desert Resorts Convention and Visitors Bureau)

call for more information. 1342 Camino Del Mar, Del Mar, CA 92014. 619/481-6225.

✪ Mountain High Balloons. Scenic flights over the Sierra Nevada north of Lake Tahoe. The cost depends on the type of flight you want. Call for rates. P.O. Box 1556, Tahoe City, CA 95730. 619/583-6292.

❋ BICYCLE TRIPS

❋ Backroads Bicycle Touring. This first-class outfit runs bicycle tours of the wine country, the Sierra foothills, the California coast, and other regions. The rides range from weekends to weeklong and include bicycle-camping tours and bicycle-inn trips with stops in historic inns and hotels. The cost is about $100 per person per day, and includes food and lodging. Bicycles and transportation are extra. P.O. Box 1626-M48, San Leandro, CA 94577. 415/895-1783.

❋ On the Loose. This Bay Area outfitter offers two- to seven-day bicycle tours of the Napa Valley, the Monterey Peninsula, Lake Tahoe, and the Big Sur. Riders cover 20 to 75 miles a day. Rates range from $150 for two days to about $800 for a week, and include everything. 1400 Shattuck Avenue, Space 7, Box 55, Berkeley, CA 94709. 415/527-4005.

❋ CATTLE/HORSE DRIVES

❋ Mammoth Lakes Pack Outfit. Every June, Lou Roeser drives his herd of horses from the Owens Valley to Mammoth Lakes, where he conducts summer pack trips. You can join the drive, which lasts three to four days and involves long hours in the saddle. At night, when the herd stops, the chuckwagon cooks the grub and songs are sung around the campfire. You will need a sleeping bag. The cost is about $125 a day. P.O. Box 61, Mammoth Lakes, CA 93546. 619/934-2434.

❋ McGee Creek Pack Station. The Ketcham family welcomes visiting riders in October when they move their herd of horses the

75 miles from McGee Canyon to Independence. It's a four-day ride. The cost is about $250 a person, and horses, saddles, and food are included. Bring a sleeping bag. Route 1, Box 162, Mammoth Lakes, CA 93546. Att: The Ketchams. 619/936-4324. (From November through May, Star Route 1, Box 100-AT, Independence, CA 93526. 619/878-2207.)

✪ Rock Creek Cow Camps. Spend four days in early May working with real cowboys on a cattle ranch in the Sierra. Everything from rounding the cows up to branding is part of the week. Bring a sleeping bag. Tents and meals provided. The cost is about $400 per rider. Box 248, Bishop, CA 93514. 619/935-4493 (October through June 619/872-8331).

✪ CANOEING/KAYAKING

✪ Burke's Canoe Trips. Leisurely 10-mile trips down the Russian River from Forestville, then return on a shuttle van. The costs vary according to time of year. P.O. Box 602, Forestville, CA 95436. 707/887-1222.

✪ California Rivers. "Kayaking for Timid Souls" is the name of the beginner's course at this northern California outfitter. The one-day trip on the Russian River covers 14 miles and costs about $50 per person. Longer trips from two to four days explore the Eel, Trinity, and Klamath rivers. The cost is about $75 per day. P.O. Box 1140, Windsor, CA 95492. 707/838-7787.

✪ Lost Horizons Sea Kayaking. Half- and multiday trips along the Californian coastline, with experienced guides and a gourmet cook. Costs depend on the trip you want. Call for rates. 190 First Street, P.O. Box 333, Avila Beach, CA 93424. 805/595-7244.

❂ GOLD PANNING

❂ Hidden Treasure Gold Mine Tours. Experience the fever that drove men wild during the gold rush days as you seek the mother lode. Costs vary. P.O. Box 28, Columbia State Park, CA 95310. 209/532-9693.

❂ HELICOPTER/AIRPLANE TOURS

❂ National Air. Charter helicopter tours over any region of the state. Costs depend on length of flight. Call for rates. 3760 Glenn Curtis, San Diego, CA 92123. 619/279-4595.

❂ Otis Spunkmeyers Sentimental Journeys DC-3 Sky Tours. It has a long name, but this company offers tours of the San Francisco Bay Area in a restored DC-3, the classic old lady of the skies. The ambiance is out of the 1940s, the seating is first class, the drinks are cold, and the snacks hot. Cost depends on length of flight. Call for costs. 14390 Catalina Street, San Leandro, CA 94577. 415/667-3800.

❂ HORSEBACK RIDES

❂ American Wilderness Experience. This experienced outfitter offers five- and seven-day rides into the Sierra Nevada. The fishing is great and the scenery is so dramatic that Ansel Adams photographed it extensively. The cost ranges from $435 to $665 per person and includes everything. P.O. Box 1486, Boulder, CO 80306. 800/444-0099 nationwide.

❂ MOUNTAINEERING

❂ Palisade School of Mountaineering. This intense program of rock- and ice-climbing is offered in the Palisades, the stunning region of the Sierra Nevada that overlooks the Owens Valley. Course offerings vary from two-day basic rock climbing to six-day advanced mountaineering. The costs begin at about $150 per person. P.O. Box 694A, Bishop, CA 93514. 619/873-5037.

✪ RIVER RUNNING

✪ Action Adventurers Wet 'n Wild. Shoot the rapids on the American, Salmon, Klamath, or Merced rivers with this experienced outfitter. The trips last up to six days and cost from $50 to $200 a day, but include everything. Box 13846, Sacramento, CA 95953. 916/662-5431 and 800/238-3688 in California.

✪ American River Touring Association. This outfitter runs oar-powered and motorized trips on seven of the state's wildest rivers. The trips last from four days to more than a week. The cost is about $100 a day. Bring sleeping gear. 445 High Street, Oakland, CA 94601. 415/465-9355.

✪ Kern River Tours. The tours start with mule trips into the canyons from the Kern, Merced, and American flow. The tours last from 1 hour to 2 days and cost from about $20 to $400 per person, depending on the tour selected. P.O. Box 3444, Lake Isabella, CA 93240. 619/379-4616.

✪ Libra Expeditions. This river run starts with a motorcoach pickup in the Los Angeles area, a night camping out in Gold Rush Country, and then a two-day run down the South Fork of the American River. The rates are $150 to $200 per person and include all meals, guides, and equipment, but not the bus. That's extra. P.O. Box 4280-A, Sunland, CA 91040. 818/352-3205.

✪ William McGinnis' Whitewater Voyages. Exhilarating runs

down the Kern, American, Carson, Merced, Klamath, and other rivers. The trips are from two to three days and cost about $100 a day and up. P.O. Box 906, El Sobrante, CA 94803. 415/222-5994.

❂ SAILING

❂ California Sailing Academy. Learn to sail or learn some of the finer points of seamanship—racing coastal piloting, celestial navigation, and more—at this Southern California school. You can start with a 14-hour beginner's class for about $200 or join a more expensive 2- to 10-day cruising course to the Channel Islands, Catalina, or Baja. 14025 Panay Way, Marina Del Rey, CA 90921. 213/821-3433.

❂ Harbor Island Sailing Club. Personalized lessons and sailboat cruises around San Diego Bay. Cost varies according to the lessons and cruises you want. Call for rates. 2040 Harbor Island Drive, San Diego, CA 92101. 619/291-9568.

❂ SOARING

❂ Calistoga Soaring Center. Fly where the only sound is that of the rushing air—in a glider spiraling ever higher above the wine country. This center offers instructions and flights. The costs vary widely. 1546 Lincoln Avenue, Calistoga, CA 94515. 707/942-5592.

❂ Fantasy Haven Airport. Lessons, rides, and rentals. 163442 Harris Road, P.O. Box 918, Tehachapi, CA 93581. 805/822-5267.

❂ TRACKING WILD MUSTANGS

❂ Rock Creek Wild Mustang Rides. The Pizona area of the Inyo National Forest is home to wild mustangs, and you can spend four days in this lovely valley tracking the mustangs and exploring the valley. The valley is filled with hot springs, Indian ruins, and wildflowers. Bring a sleeping bag. The rides are in May and early June. The cost is about $350 a rider. Box 248, Bishop, CA 93514. 619/935-4493 (October through June 619/872-8331).

Chapter Nine

A World of Festivals

California seems to have a festival celebrating every agricultural product, every ethnic group, and every historic event that took place within its borders. Here are the most entertaining, interesting, and colorful festivals held each year. In almost all cases, the dates vary from year to year, so call the number listed for this year's schedule and other details.

✪ JANUARY

✪ AT&T Pebble Beach National Pro-Am. The sensational golf courses of the Monterey Peninsula are the battleground for teams made up of top pros and celebrities. The tournament is in late January. 408/372-4711 and 800/541-9091 in California.

✪ Bob Hope Chrysler Classic. For more than three decades, this tournament has been drawing the world's top golfers. The competition is held in late January on four courses around Rancho Mirage. 619/346-8184.

❂ Palm Springs International Film Festival. Five days of premiers, seminars, and other activities in mid-January. 619/322-2930.

❂ San Francisco Ethnic Dance Festival Auditions. More than 100 ethnic dance companies representing the cultures of Asia, Africa, Europe, the Pacific Islands, the Mideast, and the Caribbean are auditioning for the festival in June. The auditions are fun and open to the public at this mid-January event. 415/474-3914.

❂ Tournament of Champions. Winners of PGA events during the previous year compete for a purse of $1 million. The tournament is held in early January at La Costa Hotel & Spa in Carlsbad. 619/438-9111.

❂ Tournament of Roses Parade. The annual New Year's Day parade in Pasadena with scores of floats, bands, and marchers. The Rose Bowl follows the parade. 818/449-4100.

❂ U.S. Men's Pro Ski Tour. This annual event held in late January at the Snow Summit Ski Resort at Big Bear Lake draws the world's top skiers. 714/866-5766.

❂ FEBRUARY

❂ Chinese New Year Celebration. The largest Asian population outside Asia marks the new year in San Francisco with an elaborate nighttime parade, food, dance, music, and martial arts at this early February event. 415/391-2000. Other large new year celebrations are in Los Angeles (213/617-0396) and San Diego (619/234-4447).

✪ Cruises and music highlight the Valhalla Festival of Art and Music on Lake Tahoe. (Courtesy of Lake Tahoe Visitors Authority)

✪ **Mardi Gras.** San Luis Obispo celebrates with a parade and evening dance in late February. 805/543-1323.

✪ **Mardi Gras Jazz Festival.** More than a dozen Dixieland bands play all over Pismo Beach in this late February celebration. 805/773-4382 and 800/443-7778 in California.

✪ **Monterey County Hot Air Fair.** This festival in late February features more than 50 hot-air balloons, food, bands, arts and crafts, and other entertainment. 408/424-7644.

✪ **Mumbo Gumbo Mardis Gras.** A Cajun celebration with a parade, masked ball, food, and entertainment in early February in San Luis Obispo. 800/634-1414 in California.

✪ Shearson-Lehman Hutton Open. Top pro golfers are teamed with celebrities for a day at this PGA tournament in mid-February in San Diego. 619/281-4653.

✪ Tet Vietnamese New Year Festival. The Vietnamese community of San Jose celebrates the Feast of the First Day, a festival to mark the start of a new year, at this early February event. 408/453-3363.

✪ MARCH

✪ Dixieland Monterey. Top Dixieland jazz musicians and groups perform at a number of locations in Monterey in early March. 408/443-5260.

✪ Fort Bragg Whaler Beer Fest. Microbreweries from all over the state take part in a beer-tasting competition and the local restaurants vie for the best chowder in this mid-March event. 707/964-3153.

✪ Mendocino Whale Festival. A celebration of the annual migration of the gray whales, with whale-watching cruises, food, art exhibits, and other entertainment at this mid-March event. 707/964-3153.

✪ Monterey Wine Festival. More than 200 wineries take part in this festival in mid-March in Monterey. Call 408/649-1770 and 800/525-3378 nationwide.

✪ Nabisco Dinah Shore LPGA Championship. The women stars of the pro golf tour join with celebrities in this late March/early April tournament in Rancho Mirage. 619/324-4546.

✪ Old Spanish Trail Days. The Old West comes to life with a trail ride, hayrides, nature hikes, and other activities in Tecopa in mid-March. 619/852-4524.

✪ Snowfest. The largest winter carnival in the West is spread over 10 days and takes place in Tahoe City and Truckee in early March. 916/583-7625.

✪ Spring Wine Show. Forty wineries take part in this tasting competition in late March and early April in Lodi. 209/369-2771.

✪ Swallows Return to San Juan Capistrano. March 19 is the date for the annual return of the swallows from their winter in Argentina to the mission. 714/493-1111.

✪ APRIL

✪ California Carrot Festival. Carrots in costumes, cakes, and as decorations mark this agricultural celebration in early April in Bakersfield. 805/323-2830.

✪ Cherry Blossom Festival. Japanese dancing, music, and food mark the blooming of the cherry trees in San Francisco. The festival is held on two weeks in late April. 415/563-2313.

✪ Columbia Wine Tasting Festival. More than 40 wineries take part in this late April competition in the historic gold rush city of Columbia. 209/532-1479.

✪ Desert Dixieland Jazz Fest. Three days and nights of Dixieland in late April in Cathedral City. 619/321-5277.

✪ Presidio Days. A three-day celebration of Santa Barbara's Spanish heritage, with dancing, food, and music. The event is held in mid- to late April. 805/966-9719.

✪ Renaissance Pleasure Faire. This re-creation of life, food, and entertainment in sixteenth-century England is a lively event on weekends from late April to early June in San Bernardino. 714/880-6211 and 800/669-8336.

✪ Round-Up Rodeo and Parade. The largest two-day rodeo in northern California, in late April in Red Bluff. 916/527-6620 and 800/545-3500 in California.

✪ Sacramento Valley Highland Games. Bagpipes, Scottish athletic contests, dancing, music, crafts, and food in this late April weekend festival in Sacramento. 916/863-0727.

✪ Santa Barbara County Vintners Festival. A tasting competition by the 23 wineries in the county, held in late April in Solvang. 805/688-0881.

✪ Shasta Dixieland Jazz Festival. Three days and three nights of music from the best Dixieland jazz bands from around the nation and Europe in this early April celebration in Redding. 916/225-4100.

✪ Victorian Home Tour. A self-guided walking tour of selected homes in Pacific Grove in late April. 408/373-3304.

✪ **MAY**

✪ Berkeley Symphony Wine and Food Tasting. A day of classic music and wonderful wines and food in early May. 415/841-2800.

✪ Cajun Crawfish Festival. The best gumbo and Grammy winners are the stars at this celebration of music and crawfish. The festival is in early May in Fairfield and usually features top entertainers. 916/361-1309.

✪ Calico Spring Festival. The desert ghost town comes to life with bluegrass, clogging, 1880s games, and other doings at this mid-May celebration. 619/254-2122.

✪ California Wine Expo. More than 50 wineries take part in this expo in early May in Redondo Beach. 213/376-6911.

✪ Calaveras County Fair and Jumping Frog Contest. Inspired by Mark Twain's classic tale of a jumping frog competition, this May contest in Angels Camp in Gold Country is serious business. 209/736-4444.

✪ Carlsbad Village Fair. More than 600 artisans take part in this huge street fair in early May. 619/931-8400.

✪ Carnival. A West Coast Mardi Gras, with parades, music, dance, and food in late May in San Francisco. 415/826-1401.

✪ Central Coast Highlands Gathering of the Clans. A traditional Scottish gathering, with games, contests, music, and food, in early May in San Luis Obispo. 805/541-8000.

✪ Cinco de Mayo Festival. Mexican dancing, food, music, and other activities at this traditional celebration in San Diego held on or near the fifth of May. 619/296-3161. Other Cinco de Mayo Festivals are held in Santa Barbara (805/965-8581), Los Angeles (213/628-3562), San Diego (619/296-3161), and San Francisco (415/826-1401).

✪ Dixieland Jazz Jubilee. The world's largest, with more than 100 bands from around the world, in late May in Sacramento. 916/372-5277.

✪ Fiesta de las Artes. This three-day festival in late May in Hermosa Beach features more than 400 booths featuring arts and crafts, fine food, and entertainment. 213/376-0951.

✪ Gold Country Jazz Festival. More than 25 bands, food, and crafts in Auburn in late May. 916/885-0432.

✪ Mendocino Coast Food and Wine Fest. A celebration of the grape and the gourmet in Mendocino in mid-May. 707/964-3153.

✪ Native American Pow Wow. Tribes from more than 30 states meet to show off dances, food, and crafts in late May in Hollister. 408/637-0051 and 800/548-3813 in California.

✪ Paso Robles Wine Festival. The region's 24 wineries join in a tasting competition in late May. 805/238-0506.

✪ Los Ranchos Visitadores. A traditional blessing of the riders of the annual cattle drive at Old Mission Santa Inez, held in early May in Solvang. 805/688-0701.

✪ Russian River Wine Festival. Tastings, food, and other entertainment in Healdsburg in mid-May. 707/433-6935 and 800/648-9922 in California.

✪ Temecula Balloon and Wine Festival. More than 60 hot-air balloons will fly in this late May party that features wine, jazz, and other activities. 714/676-4713.

✪ Tiburon Wine Festival. Fifty wineries, plus food and music at this late May celebration. 415/435-5633.

✪ JUNE

✪ American Indian Music Festival. Native-American performers and musicians, with traditional drummers and singers in this late June festival in Oakland. 415/425-1235.

✪ Huck Finn's Jubilee. Relive the days of Huck and the guys with this celebration featuring a fishing derby, fence-painting contest, a circus, and more in mid-June in Victorville. 714/780-8810.

✪ Jenner Art and Wine Festival. Taste the wines, admire the art, and have a good time at this weekend festival in late June in Jenner. 707/869-9478 and 800/253-8800 in California.

✪ Jenner Festival of the Arts. Fine arts and talented craftspersons join area wineries for this celebration in June. 707/539-6887 and 800/253-8800 in California.

✪ Klamath Salmon Festival. A Native-American event featuring salmon barbecue, logging competition, and other entertainment in mid-June in Crescent City. 707/482-5613.

✪ Lake County Wine and Food Renaissance. Annual gourmet food and wine competition in late June in Lakeport. 707/263-6658 and 800/525-3743 in California.

✪ Los Angeles Jewish Festival. A celebration of Jewish life and culture and a commemoration of the creation of the state of Israel, held in early June. 213/938-2531.

✪ Lumber Jubilee. Logging events, parade, and other lumbering games at this late June festival in Tuolumne. 209/928-4941.

✪ Paul Masson Concert Series. Jazz, blues, pop, and folk at this series of concerts in late June in Saratoga. 408/741-5181.

✪ Mission Festival and Barbecue. Enjoy a fiesta and barbecue at San Juan Bautista, the largest active mission in the state. 408/623-2127.

✪ Monterey Bay Blues Festival. The best blues by the beautiful bay in late June in Monterey. 408/649-6544.

✪ Napa Valley Wine Auction. Major wine sales event in St. Helena in June. The auction features tastings, tours, and open houses. 707/963-5246.

✪ Navato Art and Wine Festival. More than 200 artists, wines from more than 40 wineries, and other entertainment make this weekend festival in late June a popular event. 415/897-1164.

✪ Ojai Music Festival. For more than 40 years this festival has attracted some of the most distinguished conductors and musicians in the nation. The three days of concerts are in early June in Ojai. 805/646-2094.

✪ Ojai Wine Festival. Sample wines from 45 wineries, and enjoy food, music, and other entertainment at this early June event. 805/646-5501.

✪ San Francisco Ethnic Dance Festival. More than two dozen ethnic dance companies from around the world perform in this festival over three weekends in June. 415/474-3914.

✪ Sunnyvale Art and Wine Festival. More than 450 top artists from around the nation show their creations at this two-day festival in early June in Sunnyvale. 408/736-4971.

✪ JULY

✪ Carmel Bach Festival. Three weeks of the works of Johann Sebastian Bach in Carmel. 408/624-1521.

✪ Central Coast Renaissance Fair. A re-creation of an Elizabethan village, complete with food, crafts, and entertainment. The fair is held in late July in San Luis Obispo. 805/528-4427.

✪ Central Coast Wine Festival. Thirty area wineries take part in this event in late July in San Luis Obispo. 805/543-1323 and 800/643-1313 in California.

✪ A Connoisseur's Marketplace. Fine foods, great wines, 200 juried arts and crafts booths, and other attractions make this late July festival in Menlo Park an exceptional street fair. 415/325-2818.

✪ Festival of Arts and Pageant of the Masters. More than 150 artists show their creations while live models re-create the works of great artists in this six-week festival in Laguna Beach from early July to late August. 714/484-1145.

✪ Fremont Art and Wine Festival. More than 600 artisans, 20 wineries, and other entertainment make this a special event in late July. 415/657-1355.

✪ Gilroy Garlic Festival. Gourmet chefs, 200 garlic-themed booths, and continuous entertainment in late July. 408/842-1625.

✪ Lake Tahoe Summer Music Festival. Classical music and opera in a week of concerts in late July in North Lake Tahoe. 916/583-7625.

✪ Mendocino Music Festival. Musicians from the San Francisco Symphony and San Francisco Ballet Orchestra join local musicians for 10 days of concerts in mid-July. 707/544-2044.

✪ Old Spanish Days. Santa Barbara celebrates its heritage in this five-day festival in late July and early August. 805/962-8101.

✪ San Luis Obispo Mozart Festival. A week of Mozart in late July and early August. 805/543-4580.

✪ Shakespeare at Benbow Lake. A professional Bay Area troupe presents a week of the Bard at Benbow Lake State Park in Garberville. 707/923-2613.

✪ Valhalla Festival of Art and Music. Jazz, bluegrass, and chamber music in and around historic mansions of South Lake Tahoe. The concerts are in mid-July through early September. 916/544-5050.

✪ Wine Country Film Festival. A showcase of independent films from around the world, with wine tastings and food celebrations. This event takes place over 10 days in late July in Petaluma. 707/996-2536.

✪ AUGUST

✪ California State Fair. One of the largest in the nation, with rides, music, agricultural exhibits, and name entertainment from mid-August through Labor Day. 916/924-2000.

✪ Great Gatsby Festival. Antique and classic cars and boats, plus Dixieland music, dancing, hot-air balloons, and barbecue on a weekend in mid-August in South Lake Tahoe. 916/544-5050.

✪ Hoope White Deerskin Dance. A spiritual ceremonial dance performed for good luck in the odd number years in Hoope. 916/625-4211.

✪ Lake Tahoe Summer Music Festival. Classical music and opera in a week of concerts in late August in North Lake Tahoe. 916/583-7625.

✪ Los Angeles International Jazz Festival. A celebration of L.A.'s birthday with a week of jazz concerts and dance performances in late August. 213/469-5589.

✪ Sonoma County Wineries Showcase and Auction. A weekend of grand food, great wines, dancing, and music in Santa Rosa in mid-August. 707/579-0577.

✪ Starlight Jazz Festival. Two weeks of outdoor jazz concerts in South Lake Tahoe. The concerts are from mid-August to early September. 916/544-5050.

✪ SEPTEMBER

✪ Paul Bunyan Days. Logging competitions, a parade, flower show, and crafts are featured at this Labor Day weekend festival in Fort Bragg. 707/964-3153.

✪ California Indian Days. A three-day celebration of the historical and cultural contribution of Native Americans with exhibitions, dancing, crafts, and other entertainment. The festival is in late August in Roseville. 916/920-0285.

✪ Lodi Grape Festival and Wine Show. This country fair features wine tastings, home arts, and other entertainment and exhibits in mid-September. 209/369-2771.

✪ Monterey Jazz Festival. Five concerts and exhibits in late September. 408/373-3366.

✪ Valley of the Moon Vintage Festival. Grape stomping contests, food, wine tastings, and more in late September in Sonoma. 707/966-2109.

✪ Winesong. More than 90 wineries and 30 restaurants take part in this grand festival in early September in Fort Bragg. 707/964-5185.

✪ OCTOBER

✪ Festival 2000. A multicultural festival with more than 50 events of performing and visual arts over three weeks in San Francisco. 415/864-4237.

✪ Morro Bay Harbor Festival. A celebration of sealife, the fishing industry, seafood, and wines in early October in Morro Bay. 805/772-1155 and 800/231-0592 in California.

✪ NOVEMBER

✪ Calico Fine Arts Festival. About 80 famous southwestern artists display their creations in this desert ghost town in early November. 619/254-2122.

✪ Carlsbad Village Fair. More than 600 exhibitors, from all nationalities, make this early November event exciting. 619/931-8400.

✪ Death Valley 49ers Encampment. It's not the training camp of the football team. No, this early November festival in Death Valley is the re-creation of the fateful crossing of the valley by the pioneers of 1849, with music, art, hikes, and other entertainment. 619/852-4524.

✪ Doo-Dah Parade. Zany marching units include the Briefcase Brigade and the Kazoo Marching Band. These and other crazed persons put the fun into this late November ritual in Pasadena. 818/796-2591.

✪ DECEMBER

✪ Christmas in the Adobes. A candlelight tour of Monterey's historic district in mid-December. 408/649-7110.

✪ San Diego Parade of Lights. Boats, all decorated with Christmas lights, parade past the waterfront in late December. 619/222-0561.

✪ Victorian Christmas. A blending of Hispanic and Victorian Christmas traditions, with tours of the historic Dallidet Adobe in San Luis Obispo. 805/541-8000.

Index